WOMEN AND THE MILITARY

MARTIN BINKIN *and* SHIRLEY J. BACH

WOMEN AND THE MILITARY

THE BROOKINGS INSTITUTION
Washington, D.C.

Copyright © 1977 by
THE BROOKINGS INSTITUTION
1775 Massachusetts Avenue, N.W., Washington, D.C. 20036

Library of Congress Cataloging in Publication Data:
Binkin, Martin, 1928–
    Women and the military.
    (Studies in defense policy)
    Includes bibliographical references.
    1. United States—Armed Forces—Women.
2. Women—-Employment—United States. 3. Women's
rights—United States. I. Bach, Shirley J., joint
author. II. Title. III. Series.
UB323.B57   331.4'81'35500973   77-24040
ISBN 0-8157-0966-8
ISBN 0-8157-0965-X pbk.

9 8 7 6 5 4 3 2 1

THE BROOKINGS INSTITUTION is an independent organization devoted to nonpartisan research, education, and publication in economics, government, foreign policy, and the social sciences generally. Its principal purposes are to aid in the development of sound public policies and to promote public understanding of issues of national importance.

The Institution was founded on December 8, 1927, to merge the activities of the Institute for Government Research, founded in 1916, the Institute of Economics, founded in 1922, and the Robert Brookings Graduate School of Economics and Government, founded in 1924.

The Board of Trustees is responsible for the general administration of the Institution, while the immediate direction of the policies, program, and staff is vested in the President, assisted by an advisory committee of the officers and staff. The by-laws of the Institution state: "It is the function of the Trustees to make possible the conduct of scientific research, and publication, under the most favorable conditions, and to safeguard the independence of the research staff in the pursuit of their studies and in the publication of the results of such studies. It is not a part of their function to determine, control, or influence the conduct of particular investigations or the conclusions reached."

The President bears final responsibility for the decision to publish a manuscript as a Brookings book. In reaching his judgment on the competence, accuracy, and objectivity of each study, the President is advised by the director of the appropriate research program and weighs the views of a panel of expert outside readers who report to him in confidence on the quality of the work. Publication of a work signifies that it is deemed a competent treatment worthy of public consideration but does not imply endorsement of conclusions or recommendations.

The Institution maintains its position of neutrality on issues of public policy in order to safeguard the intellectual freedom of the staff. Hence interpretations or conclusions in Brookings publications should be understood to be solely those of the authors and should not be attributed to the Institution, to its trustees, officers, or other staff members, or to the organizations that support its research.

FOREWORD

The U.S. armed forces employ some two million people, yet by 1982, according to the Pentagon, only 7 percent of them will be women. Is this proportion practical in light of today's changing social mores and the diminishing prospects of attracting qualified male volunteers? There are now over a million single women in the labor force aged eighteen or nineteen, about one-third of whom could be expected to meet the services' most stringent entrance requirements. The Pentagon plans to recruit only about 30,000—because laws and policies largely relegate women to traditional or minor roles.

Sooner or later the nation will have to decide whether such laws and policies should be changed and, if so, how. The issue is important and controversial; its resolution could have significant social, economic, and military implications.

In this study, the sixteenth in the Brookings Studies in Defense Policy series, Martin Binkin and Shirley J. Bach set forth the rationale for changing the sex composition of U.S. military forces in light of social attitudes and national security concerns. They argue that present restrictions deny women access to significant jobs and deny the nation a pool of competent workers who might be willing to volunteer. But they recognize that the consequences of removing all barriers, especially the prohibition against assigning women to combat duty, are not yet well enough understood to assess their influence on military effectiveness or society as a whole. Nonetheless, they outline what can be done within the present statutory framework to expand the military role of women. They also describe the implications of changing the present framework so as to expand the role of women still further.

Martin Binkin, a senior fellow in the Brookings Foreign Policy Studies program who was formerly with the Office of the Assistant Secretary of Defense for Systems Analysis, has written extensively on defense manpower issues. Lieutenant Colonel Shirley J. Bach, now returned to active duty with the U.S. Air Force, was a Brookings Federal Executive Fellow in 1975–76.

The authors thank Major General Jeanne M. Holm (U.S. Air Force, retired) and Professor George H. Quester of Cornell University for their helpful comments. During the course of the study, the authors received useful data and assistance from numerous officials in the Office of the Secretary of Defense and in the military services. They are particularly indebted to the following organizations: U.S. Army Research Institute for the Behavioral and Social Sciences; the Office of the Director, Women's Army Corps; the Manpower Research and Data Analysis Center and the Office of the Coordinator for Women in the Services—both in the Office of the Assistant Secretary of Defense for Manpower and Reserve Affairs; the Bureau of Naval Personnel; and the Navy Personnel Research and Development Center. They benefited greatly from many comments on drafts of the manuscript, especially from those of John F. Ahearne, Judie Armington, Nancy J. Hampson, Richard W. Hunter, Arthur Pearce Leary, Charles C. Moskos, Jr., Gary R. Nelson, Thomas K. Newell, Jr., Jane C. Record, and Mary Douglas Young.

They are also grateful to their Brookings colleagues Barry M. Blechman, Robert W. Hartman, H. James Miller, Henry Owen, and Frederick Young for valuable suggestions; to Mary M. F. Delashmit, who translated material from the Soviet literature; to Penelope Harpold, whose meticulous attention to detail minimized the risk of factual error; and to Ann M. Ziegler, who so ably carried the secretarial burden.

The authors especially appreciate the contribution of Barbara P. Haskins, who not only edited the manuscript but improved its substance by drawing upon her first-hand experience as a seaman-torpedoman in the Women's Royal Naval Service in the Second World War.

The Institution gratefully acknowledges the assistance of the Ford Foundation, whose grant helps to support its work in defense studies. The views expressed herein are those of the authors and should not be ascribed to the persons who provided data or who commented on the manuscript, to the Ford Foundation, or to the trustees, officers, or other staff members of the Brookings Institution.

BRUCE K. MAC LAURY
President

June 1977
Washington, D.C.

CONTENTS

Tables

Figures

WOMEN AND THE MILITARY

CHAPTER ONE

INTRODUCTION

In many ways, the character and composition of a nation's military system mirror the society that it is established to protect and defend. Thus it comes as no surprise that the armed forces of the United States should now face a period of great uncertainty, at once under pressure to remain apace of the fundamental changes taking place in American society but at the same time understandably cautious about breaking with deeply rooted military traditions. Vividly illustrating this dilemma is the controversial question of the role of women in the changing military establishment.

Although, since the turn of the century, women have served intermittently in the armed forces of the United States, with the exception of the Second World War their participation has been relatively restricted. From the mid-forties to the early seventies they constituted less than 2 percent of total military strength and were confined largely to health care and administrative occupations. The draft provided an abundant source of manpower and defense planners had little incentive to attract female recruits. Traditional attitudes as to women's "proper place" persisted, and there was little agitation for change. In short, women's status in the military was not a live issue.

That state of affairs did not last, however. First, the changing lifestyles of women and the tide of feminism that swept the nation in the late sixties culminated in congressional approval of the Equal Rights Amendment and altered common perspectives of women's place in American society. Second, the decision to abolish conscription meant that male recruits could no longer be viewed as a "free good"; the military had to compete for manpower in the marketplace.

Thus, under pressure from the women's movement, on the one hand, and facing possible shortages of male volunteers, on the other, the Pentagon decided in 1972 that the scope of women's participation had to be expanded and the many sources of sex discrimination removed. At that time there were about 45,000 females in the services, 1.9 percent of all military personnel. By 1976, close to 110,000 women constituted over 5 percent of the uniformed work force.

For this expansion to take place women had to be assigned to a greater variety of jobs, most particularly at the enlisted level; there was no fear of a shortfall in officers who were less affected by the end of the draft. Traditionally, enlisted women had largely been confined to health care and clerical duties in peacetime. In fact, before the 1972 expansion, only 35 percent of all military enlisted occupations were open to women; by 1976 over 80 percent were open. The proportion actually assigned to the new kinds of nontraditional jobs also increased: 10 percent of all females in the armed forces were assigned to scientific, technical, or blue-collar labor specialties in 1972, whereas in 1976 the proportion was over 40 percent.

But this expansion is largely over *if* present laws and policies persist. The high rate of increase in the total number of females that occurred during the first half of the 1970s, averaging about 20 percent annually, started to abate in fiscal 1976. Annual growth of female strength is expected to average about 5 percent a year through fiscal 1982, at which time about 147,000 women will constitute about 7 percent of the armed forces.

If these goals are to be exceeded, either Congress will have to change certain laws or the military services will have to alter certain policies that circumscribe women's opportunities. Women in the Navy and Air Force, for instance, are prohibited by law from serving on ships or on aircraft engaged in combat missions. Basing their own policies on the premise that this nation does not condone the use of women in direct combat roles, the Army and Marine Corps bar women from serving with units that might come face to face with the enemy. In addition, some non-combat jobs are specifically reserved for men so as not to impede their career development and to give them a respite from combat or arduous duty. Whether these laws and policies should be changed and, if so, how they should be changed are important issues whose resolution could have significant social and economic as well as military implications.

At one extreme, maintaining the status quo denies to women a full measure of equality and responsibility. Moreover, by overlooking this large reservoir of labor, military planners run the risk of having to either unnecessarily increase monetary incentives or reinstitute the draft in order to maintain the present size and quality of the armed forces. At the other extreme, removing all legislative and policy constraints based on sex (including those against using women in combat) runs counter to long-standing cultural mores and has uncertain implications for military effectiveness.

Caught in a crossfire of ideologies, this emotional question has so far escaped objective scrutiny and informed public debate. This analysis attempts to increase public awareness of the issues involved and to promote a better understanding of the costs and benefits of policy change.

After tracing the evolution of the role of women in the armed forces, the study examines the rationales currently underlying the military services' programs for women.

The social issues are then discussed; first, from the individual woman's perspective—what has she to gain from military service?—and, second, from society's point of view—how do the public, Congress, the judiciary, and the military itself view a more active, less traditional role for women in the military establishment? In all debates on these issues there is the continuing conflict between the drive for equal rights and the traditional feelings, deeply rooted in American culture, that the defense of the nation is the responsibility of men.

Next, the national security issues are examined: first, from the budgetary standpoint—what are the relative costs of recruiting and sustaining men and women?—and, second, in terms of military effectiveness—how would an expanded rate of recruitment for women influence the capabilities of military units? Consideration is given to the possible conflict between the budgetary advantages of increasing reliance on women and the possible risks to national security because of the uncertain implications for military effectiveness.

Against this background the study concludes with proposals to move toward an optimum utilization of enlisted women in the military; it attempts to strike a balance among the competing social forces and among competing national security factors.

CHAPTER TWO

LOOKING BACK

Traditionally, service in the military establishment of the United States, as in those of most other nations, has been a masculine calling. Except as nurses, the formal association of women in the military is a relatively recent phenomenon. Indeed, serious interest in defining women's role in the armed forces did not awaken until World War II, and it was not until 1948 that women achieved permanent military status. The changing role of women in large part mirrors their changing role in American society. Even more recently it has been influenced by military necessity.

Before Pearl Harbor: This Man's Army

Before Pearl Harbor, American peacetime military forces were generally small and relatively unskilled cadres. Partly because of these characteristics and partly because of prevailing social attitudes, they were almost exclusively male—the exploits of Molly Pitcher and other legendary women warriors notwithstanding.[1]

In contrast to contemporary military institutions, which are equipped with increasingly sophisticated weaponry demanding less physical prowess and larger support infrastructures, the earlier standing armies were composed mainly of foot-slogging riflemen whose primary function was to engage the enemy with small arms or in hand-to-hand combat and who had few logistical requirements. Since the military had little need for the types of occupational skills that Victorian concepts of propriety permitted

---

1. Molly Pitcher (whose real name was Mary Ludwig Hays McCauley) is reported to have assumed the duties of her wounded husband as a cannoneer in the Revolutionary War. See Norma Olin Ireland, *Index to Women of the World* (Faxon, 1970), pp. xxxi, 414.

women to pursue—and few ventured to question the traditional view that fighting wars was man's work—the absence of women in the military ranks is not difficult to understand.

This is not to say, however, that women did not participate in military action. Disguised as men, small numbers of women served in a combat role in every war before the twentieth century in which the United States became involved; among the most well known are Deborah Sampson ("Robert Shurtleff") in the Revolutionary War, Lucy Brewer ("George Baker") in the War of 1812, and Loreta Velasquez ("Harry T. Buford") in the Civil War.[2] Less publicized have been the countless women who served, albeit in a civilian status, as nurses, cooks, laundresses, seamstresses, and in other acceptable feminine pursuits. With the turn of the century came the first uniformed military women; the Army Nurse Corps was set up in 1901 followed by the Navy Nurse Corps in 1908. But neither group received full military status, equal pay, or equal benefits until World War II.

In the wake of nineteenth century industrialism, American women developed skills that were to become increasingly relevant to the military. In fact, women dominated some occupations (for example, positions as secretaries and telephone operators) that, with changes in military technology and organization, had come into greater demand by World War I.

The Army, over the protests of General Pershing, held fast to its prohibition against enlisted women; however, the Navy Department, concerned about a shortage of clerical labor in the shore establishment, enlisted about 13,000 women for service in the Navy as Yeoman-Fs, generally referred to as "yeomanettes," and in the Marine Corps as Marine-Fs, or "marinettes." These women—who worked as telephone operators, clerical workers, typists, and stenographers—were the first to be accorded full military rank and status.[3] Following the First World War, however, they were demobilized, and with the exception of the nurse corps the American armed services were once again all-male institutions.

The question of women in the military apparently attracted little serious

2. See John Laffin, *Women in Battle* (Abelard-Schuman, 1967) especially pp. 31–32 and pp. 116–24.

3. The Navy had to bend the law somewhat. According to Navy regulations, all yeomen were required to be assigned to a ship, but women were prohibited from serving on ships. To solve this problem, all women in the service were assigned to a tugboat permanently buried in the mud of the Potomac River. See Patricia J. Thomas, "Utilization of Enlisted Women in the Military" (San Diego, Calif.: Navy Personnel Research and Development Center, 1975; processed), p. 4.

attention between the World Wars. However, two studies during the period are worth noting. The first, written under the auspices of Anita Phipps, the Army's director of women's relations (a civilian liaison post), proposed that a "women's service corps" be formed as an integral part of the Army. According to her plan, women should be "fully trained and assigned only in units under the command of women officers, with not less than a squad at any station and no individual billeting allowed." This plan was rejected by the Army General Staff in 1926.[4]

A second study—called the Hughes Plan after its architect Major Everett S. Hughes—was based on the premise that women would inevitably play a role in future conflicts and recommended that women serving overseas or in danger zones be militarized. It also advocated that women be integrated into the men's army, with similar uniforms and privileges. The study was sent to the Army chief of staff in 1928 and again in 1930. Its fate was described as follows:

> A dejected-looking sheaf of handwritten scraps of paper indicated that the studies were carried back and forth from G-1 [Personnel] to the Chief of Staff to the Secretary of War to G-1, bearing notations of diminishing intensity, such as "Hold until Secretary of War decides"; "Hold until fall when women return to their homes after summer activities"; and, finally, merely "Hold." The last one in the series, dated 5 January 1931, stated: "General B. [Brigadier General Albert J. Bowley] says may as well suspend; no one seems willing to do anything about it."[5]

World War II: Freeing the Men to Fight

As U.S. participation in World War II began to appear inevitable, pressures increased to once again admit women into the armed forces. Military reports about the indispensable women's auxiliaries in the United Kingdom, warnings that American forces should not rely on support from these groups because of Britain's serious manpower shortages, reports that Russian and Chinese women were taking an active part in national defense (including manual labor, front-line duty, and other tasks traditionally reserved for men), and demands by U.S. women's organizations

4. This section is based largely upon Mattie E. Treadwell, *The Women's Army Corps* (Department of the Army, Office of the Chief of Military History, 1954), an excellent study of the role of women in the U.S. Army before and during World War II. The quotation is on p. 12.

5. Ibid., pp. 14–15. According to Treadwell, the study was "buried so deep in the files that [it was] recovered only after the WAAC was six months old [1942] and War Department planners had already made most of the mistakes he [Hughes] predicted."

for opportunities to serve in the defense effort all contributed to renewed interest in the part that women should play in the war effort.

Early in 1941, Representative Edith Nourse Rogers of Massachusetts was dissuaded from pursuing her plans to establish a woman's corps in the Army. The War Department insisted that the framework for a women's organization was already in the outline stage, and being developed within the Army. The Army's version—providing for a civilian auxiliary not a part of the Army—was finally introduced in the House of Representatives by Congresswoman Rogers in May 1941. The bill immediately sank from sight after being referred routinely to the Bureau of the Budget.

Pearl Harbor changed the attitude of the bill's opponents, however, and the Bureau of the Budget approved it four days later. The Women's Army Auxiliary Corps (WAAC) was created on May 14, 1942, followed two months later by the WAVES (Women Accepted for Voluntary Emergency Service). Closely on its heels came the U.S. Marine Corps Women's Reserve and the Coast Guard Women's Reserve, called the SPARs ("Semper Paratus, Always Ready"). The designation in each instance implied the temporary nature of the organizations.

World War II can justifiably be viewed as a turning point in the history of women's participation in the military. Large numbers were involved— a total of about 350,000 women served in the four services. And although the vast majority were employed in health care, administration, and communications, women demonstrated their competence in virtually every occupation outside of direct combat—they were employed as airplane mechanics, parachute riggers, gunnery instructors, air traffic controllers, naval air navigators, and the like. Some 800 women also served as Women's Airforce Service Pilots (WASPs). Although never accorded full military status, they ferried all types of military airplanes, including combat aircraft.

Military women were also employed overseas, many following closely behind the fighting forces, suffering the same sort of deprivations as men. The "first American women's expeditionary force in history"—a post headquarters company—arrived in North Africa just two months after the U.S. invasion. At one time, there were about 2,000 Army women serving in the Mediterranean theater of operations, who later followed the U.S. Fifth Army into Italy, many being stationed from twelve to thirty-five miles behind the advancing troops. By the end of the Italian campaign, most of the Wacs serving in Africa had been deployed to the Italian peninsula.

The first unit of military women reached Europe in July 1943, with the initial contingent earmarked for administrative duties at Army Air Force stations in England. Less than a year later, and after lively debate about the propriety of the action, women were deployed to France and later to Germany. The First WAC unit landed in Normandy thirty-eight days after D-Day and, by V-E Day, there were some 8,000 Wacs in Europe—about half the number requested by the theater commanders. Their performance under arduous conditions is described as follows:

In the eight months before V-E Day, WACS followed closely behind the fighting forces. Food, quarters, and supplies were the same as those available to the men. The only reported difficulty concerning quarters was the absence of heat and hot water; doctors estimated that 25 percent of the women in one unit had chilblains. Conditions were extremely unsettled, medical and hospital care uncertain; there was cold, rain, snow, and mud; it was seldom any longer possible to have advance inspection of housing. Nevertheless, the strenuousness of this period had no perceptible effect; authorities were in fact surprised to discover that the WAC sick rate was the lowest of the year. During the initial six weeks when WACS were landing on Normandy beaches, only one woman had to be sent back to England because of illness. WACS noted that after the V-bombs in England, the sound of distant artillery fire in Normany was a relief. Morale remained high in direct proportion to the woman's sense of playing an immediate and essential part in the winning of the war.[6]

Women also participated in the Pacific theater, though on a smaller scale than in Europe. Except for nurses, military women did not become involved in the war in the Southwest Pacific until 1944. Eventually, about 5,200 served there, principally in Australia, New Guinea, and the Philippines and mainly in clerical and stenographic posts. Their service earned the praise of General Douglas MacArthur:

I moved my Wacs forward early after occupation of recaptured territory because they were needed and they were soldiers in the same manner that my men were soldiers. Furthermore, if I had not moved my Wacs when I did, I would have had mutiny . . . as they were so eager to carry on where needed.[7]

Women's role in the Second World War was far more significant than is suggested by the brief review above. Perhaps the ultimate compliment paid to the American women who served was offered by Albert Speer, Adolph Hitler's weapons production chief, to Lieutenant General Ira C. Eaker, an Army Air Force commander in Europe during World War II:

How wise you were to bring your women into your military and into your labor force. Had we done that initially, as you did, it could well have affected

6. Ibid., p. 388.
7. Ibid., p. 423.

the whole course of the war. We would have found out, as you did, that women were equally effective, and for some skills, superior to males.[8]

Among the several episodes in recent history in which women have been used in combat operations, the experience of Russian women in the Soviet armed forces has been one of the most publicized. In the Soviet Union, more so than elsewhere, the war obliterated the conventional demarcation between male and female occupations.[9] The extreme shortage of manpower for military operations forced the Soviets to conscript their women. Initially, female draftees had to have medical and clerical qualifications, but as the war progressed and the Nazi war machine advanced, all childless Soviet women who were not otherwise filling vital war jobs were drafted. Reportedly, their peak strength reached the million mark, at which time women constituted about 8 percent of total Soviet military forces.[10] While many served in the rear areas to release men for combat, some saw combat duty. Most notable were the 586th Women's Aircraft Fighter Regiment, the Forty-sixth Night Bomber Regiment, and the 125th Day Bomber Regiment. Russian women also reportedly served with ground combat units as tank crewmembers, machine gunners, snipers, and artillery crewmembers. Moreover, about one of every ten partisans was a woman, many of whom served as scouts, snipers, and saboteurs. At the end of the war, the Soviet Union ended its conscription of women and demobilized most of them.[11]

8. As reported by Lieutenant General Ira C. Eaker (United States Air Force, retired), *Navy Times,* December 6, 1976. The record indicates that women in Nazi Germany were conscripted for both the military and industry during World War II with the greatest number serving in the later years of the war (1943–45). For the most part they served as noncombatants, although apparently some manned searchlights and antiaircraft batteries. For a more complete account, see: Ursula von Gersdorff, *Frauen im Kriegsdienst, 1914–1945* (Stuttgart: Deutsche Verlags-Anstalt, 1969); Hierl Konstantin, *Idea and Formation of Labor Service* (Germany: U.S. Army, Historical Division, 1946); August Schalkaeuser, *German Women in War Service during World War II* (Germany: U.S. Army, Historical Division, 1949).

9. See the appendix for further details on women's participation in the armed forces of other countries.

10. U.S. Defense Intelligence Agency, "Women in the Soviet Armed Forces," DDI-1100-109-76 (DIA, March 1976; processed).

11. The World War II exploits of many Russian women have been documented in Soviet literature. For example, Olga Yamchikova is reported to have flown ninety-three missions and eventually became a test pilot and the first Russian woman to fly jet aircraft. Valerie Khomyakova is alleged to have been the first Russian woman to destroy an enemy aircraft at night. Dubbed the "flying witch" by the Nazis because of her prowess, Soviet sources indicate that she was killed in an air battle later in the war. The extent of women's participation in the Soviet military forces, however, is a subject of some controversy. Some have speculated that the instances listed above

The Postwar Decades: Return to Apathy

With the end of the war came the largest and most rapid demobilization in U.S. history. Total military strength was reduced from a peak of 12.1 million in 1945 to about 1.4 million in 1948. Over the period, the number of women declined from 266,000 to just over 14,000, a mere 1 percent of all military personnel.[12] With the authorization for the WAC due to lapse in 1948, the few remaining in the service found themselves in limbo; about half resigned in 1947.[13]

The Women's Armed Services Integration Act of 1948[14]

This uncertainty did not last. Many forces were at work to precipitate the enactment of legislation. One was concern that without conscription the armed services would have difficulty in meeting their recruitment needs.[15] The military draft, in existence since 1940, was allowed to lapse on March 31, 1947. With inadequate male enlistments to maintain total strength levels, the armed forces viewed women as an important alternate source of supply.

Institutionalizing the role of women would also attain other objectives: it would provide a trained nucleus that would facilitate expansion of the service in a national emergency; it would economize by using women in jobs—the "feminine" occupations—for which they were considered better suited than men; and it would make it easier to determine, through experimentation, how best to utilize women in the military.[16]

---

may have been atypical and specifically chosen to dramatize the need for wartime commitment, or as "an exercise in public relations, designed to impress the outside world with the underdog position of the country in question." See George M. Quester, "Women in Combat," *International Security,* vol. 1 (Spring 1977), p. 81.

12. Department of Defense, *Selected Manpower Statistics* (Office of the Assistant Secretary of Defense [Comptroller], Directorate for Information, Operation, and Control, May 1975; processed), pp. 22, 46.

13. *Subcommittee Hearing on S. 1641 to Establish the Women's Army Corps in the Regular Army, to Authorize the Enlistment and Appointment of Women in the Regular Navy and Marine Corps and the Naval and Marine Corps Reserve, and for Other Purposes,* House Armed Services Committee, Subcommittee on Organization and Mobilization, 80:1 (Government Printing Office, 1948), p. 5595.

14. Women's Armed Services Integration Act of 1948, 62 Stat. 356–75.

15. *Women's Armed Services Integration Act of 1947,* S. Rept. 567, 80:1 (GPO, 1947), p. 4.

16. Ibid.

Few in Congress were disturbed by the Pentagon's proposals. Debate that did take place centered on two main issues—first, whether women should become an integral part of the regular military establishment or whether they should be maintained in a reserve or temporary status; and second, how many women should be allowed to enter the services.

As it happened, women were provided regular status and the Pentagon's proposal on numbers was adopted: enlisted women would not exceed 2 percent of total enlisted strength and female officers (excluding nurses) would not exceed 10 percent of female enlisted strength.[17] The rationale for these ceilings, which remained in effect for twenty years, was far from clear.

Though signifying a major breakthrough for women, the 1948 legislation also sowed the seeds of sex discrimination that were to persist for two decades. The act imposed several limitations:[18]

1. In recruitment, no woman under eighteen years of age could enlist and if under twenty-one years of age, she was required to have the written consent of her parent or guardian. In contrast, seventeen-year-old males could enlist and written consent was required only if they were under eighteen.

2. Career opportunities for women were circumscribed because none could serve in command positions or hold a permanent grade above lieutenant colonel (or commander in the Navy). One woman in each women's component could hold the rank of colonel (or captain in the Navy) for four years but she had to revert to lieutenant colonel (or commander in the Navy) upon completing that term. In practice, this temporary rank was reserved for the officer who was chief or director of her respective component.

3. Dependent benefits were similar to those of men except that husbands had to demonstrate dependency. Moreover, children were not considered dependents unless the father was deceased or the mother provided chief support.

As things turned out, conscription was reinstituted just twelve days after the Women's Armed Services Integration Act was signed, thus easing the services' concerns about recruiting shortfalls. During the early 1950s, an abortive attempt was made to recruit some 100,000 women to meet

17. 62 Stat. 357, 358. General Dwight D. Eisenhower had recommended a larger authorization and Lyndon B. Johnson, then a congressman from Texas, had advocated a ceiling of 4 percent. See *Subcommittee Hearing on S. 1641* . . . , pp. 1621–25.

18. See 62 Stat. 357, 360–61, 363, 368.

the personnel demands imposed by the Korean War.[19] But general lack of interest and the war's unpopularity doomed the effort to early failure.

Indeed, the percentage of women in the military, even including nurses, never reached the maximum authorization; from 1948 to 1969 the percentage varied between 1.0 and 1.5 percent, averaging 1.2 percent.[20] Moreover, military women reverted to "women's work"—mainly health care and clerical jobs. One participant described the situation as follows: "It would be no exaggeration to say that probably the most significant accomplishment of the women in the line of the services from 1953 to 1966 was sheer survival."[21]

Women's Role in the Sixties

Under pressures from the expanding role of women in the labor force and from the large manpower demands of the Vietnam War, the Department of Defense established a task force in 1966 to reassess the role of women in the armed forces.[22] The study group established directions in which women's programs should evolve and laid the groundwork for the expansion that was to occur several years later. Partly as a result of that study, several significant changes were made in 1967 in the status of military women. Provisions of the law that limited the career opportunities available to women officers were altered, first to allow them to hold permanent grades up through colonel (captain in the Navy) and to be appointed as general or flag officers and, second, to remove existing differences between men and women with respect to retirement provisions. The 1967 law also struck down the 2 percent limitation on female enlisted strengths that had been in effect since 1947.[23] Nevertheless, women constituted less than 2 percent of total military strength for the remainder of the decade; and if it were not for changing social mores and military expediency, that would probably still be the case today.

It was during this postwar period of relative apathy in the United States

19. Interview, February 4, 1977, with Major General Jeanne M. Holm (USAF, ret.), former director of Women in the Air Force (WAF).

20. See Department of Defense, *Selected Manpower Statistics*, pp. 22, 46.

21. From a speech by Major General Jeanne M. Holm before the 1975 spring meeting of the Defense Advisory Committee on Women in the Services, Washington, D.C., April 7, 1975 (DACOWITS, 1975; processed).

22. Department of Defense, "Report of the Inter-Service Working Group on Utilization of Women in the Armed Services" (August 31, 1966; processed).

23. 81 Stat. 374–84. The first women to achieve general officer rank were Army officers—the director, Women's Army Corps, and chief, Army Nurse Corps, both of whom were promoted to brigadier general on June 11, 1970.

that participation by women in the Israeli armed forces captured attention worldwide. This can be traced back to the Haganah—the illegal Jewish army that existed prior to the creation of the state of Israel—and it was notably evident in the Palmach—the special "commando battalions" established in 1941. By the start of the War of Liberation in 1948, according to one source, female soldiers in the Haganah constituted about 15 percent of the total. In the first phase of that war (April–May 1948), which was principally defensive guerrilla warfare carried out by company-sized units of the Haganah, women reportedly "shared in both the active and defensive battle activities." When fighting resumed in July 1948 after the aborted United Nations truce, the Israeli Army captured the initiative in a series of offensive operations. With a change in tactics and organization (the Haganah and other illegal groups had united to form the Israel Defense Forces), "there were fewer battle tasks for women to perform."[24]

A noncombat role for Israeli women was institutionalized in the postwar army. With a relatively small standing force backed up by a large reserve system, Israel established conscription for both men and women, but the laws governing the compulsory service for women are somewhat more liberal in terms of age limits, deferments, and exemptions.

Women's role, too, has evolved over the years into the more traditional Western pattern; today, combat jobs have virtually disappeared. The popularized image of the Israeli woman in battle dress, wielding a machine gun with a bandolier slung over her shoulder, has nevertheless persisted for close to three decades. Although her modern counterparts are trained in the use of light weapons, with few exceptions they do not carry or use weapons. The swing back to traditionalism has been lamented by one feminist:

> Even the Israeli woman soldier in uniform, a model of female liberation to the world, is rapidly adjusting to a new fashion. The very symbol of her equal participation in society—the soldier's uniform—has been shortened so often that it has become a miniskirt, a symbol of something quite different.[25]

The Early Seventies: The Expansion Years

With the decision in 1970 to end the draft, the United States embarked on a venture unprecedented in any nation's history: to field a military

24. The description in this paragraph is from Lionel Tiger and Joseph Shepher, *Women in the Kibbutz* (Harcourt Brace Jovanovich, 1975), p. 186. See the appendix for more detail.

25. Paula Stern, "Lib Lagging in Israel," *Washington Star-News*, July 2, 1973.

force over two million strong relying solely on volunteers. Could enough men be found, willing and able to volunteer, without exorbitant additional costs, and without compromising the quality of military manpower? Reasonable people disagreed.

Although it appreciated the great uncertainties involved, the Department of Defense realized that it had to further expand the role of women. Early in 1972, a task force established by the secretary of defense set out "to prepare contingency plans for increasing the use of women to offset possible shortages of male recruits after the end of the draft."[26]

No sooner had the study commenced than the Equal Rights Amendment cleared the Congress.[27] The vague contours of the amendment left its specific impact on the military unclear pending final ratification and judicial interpretation. However, rejection of an amendment to the ERA, which would have excluded females from the draft, suggested that Congress anticipated a significantly expanded role for women in the military.[28]

Meanwhile, the armed forces did not wait for the states to ratify the ERA before instituting changes. Many were initiated by the services, either because they perceived a genuine need or because they saw the handwriting on the wall. Also, a number of military women instigated legal challenges to a variety of military practices charging discrimination. The results of the litigation were mixed, but women achieved one major victory when the Supreme Court struck down the law, described above, which denied military women certain dependency benefits that had been made available to similarly situated male personnel.[29]

The combined impact of the ERA debate, the feminist litigation, and the end of the draft is seen in five areas.

First, despite many obstacles, there has been a substantial increase in the number of women in the armed forces. In 1972, when the decision was made to increase the proportion of women in the military, it was about 1.9 percent (some 45,000 women) of all military personnel (see table 2-1). By 1976, it was over 5 percent (108,000), and by most ac-

26. Central All-Volunteer Force Task Force, "Utilization of Military Women" (Office of the Assistant Secretary of Defense for Manpower and Reserve Affairs, December 1972; processed), p. i.

27. 86 Stat. 1523.

28. The Equal Rights Amendment states simply, but broadly: "Equality of rights under law shall not be denied or abridged by the United States or by any state on account of sex" (ibid). The attempt to amend the ERA to exempt women from the draft is discussed in chapter 5.

29. *Frontiero* v. *Richardson,* 411 U.S. 677 (1973). Because of the precedents established, this case is discussed more fully in chapter 5.

Table 2-1. Total Female Military Personnel, End of Fiscal Years 1971–76
Women in thousands

Military service and class	1971	1972	1973	1974	1975	1976
Army	16.9	16.8	20.7	30.7	42.3	48.7
Officer	5.0	4.4	4.3	4.4	4.6	4.8
Enlisted	11.8	12.3	16.5	26.3	37.7	43.9
Navy	8.8	9.4	12.6	17.0	21.2	22.7
Officer	2.9	3.2	3.5	3.6	3.6	3.5
Enlisted	5.9	6.2	9.1	13.4	17.5	19.2
Marine Corps	2.3	2.3	2.3	2.7	3.2	3.4
Officer	0.3	0.3	0.3	0.3	0.3	0.3
Enlisted	2.0	2.1	2.0	2.4	2.8	3.1
Air Force	14.9	16.5	19.8	24.2	30.2	34.2
Officer	4.7	4.8	4.7	4.8	5.0	4.8
Enlisted	10.1	11.7	15.0	19.5	25.2	29.2
Department of Defense total	42.8	45.0	55.4	74.7	96.9	108.8
Officer	12.9	12.6	12.8	13.1	13.6	13.4
Enlisted	29.9	32.4	42.6	61.6	83.3	95.4
Total number of women as percent of total military personnel	1.6	1.9	2.5	3.5	4.6	5.2

Sources: Fiscal years 1971–74, Department of Defense, *Selected Manpower Statistics* (Office of the Assistant Secretary of Defense [Comptroller], Directorate of Information, Operation, and Control, May 1975; processed), pp. 22, 46; fiscal years 1975–76, Department of Defense, "Manpower Requirements Report for Fiscal Year 1977" (February 1977; processed), pp. XVI-1, and Office of the Assistant Secretary of Defense for Manpower and Reserve Affairs, "Use of Women in the Military," background study (OASD, Manpower and Reserve Affairs, May 1977; processed), p. 5. Figures may not add to totals because of rounding.

counts now exceeds that in any other nation. Because of definitional problems and security concerns, it is difficult to make comparisons of female participation among different nations. In absolute numbers of women, there is little doubt that the United States far surpasses any other nation; the armed forces of Great Britain, its nearest rival, employs but 15,000 women. In relative terms, the proportion of women in the Israeli armed forces, although kept secret, apparently approximates that in the U.S. military establishment. But, given the trends in both nations, it is clear that the United States will soon emerge as the world's leader in women's participation in the military.[30]

Consistent with the growth in total strength has been the marked increase in the number of women entering the services each year. In contrast with 1972, when one of every thirty enlisted recruits was female, in 1976 one of every thirteen was a woman. These changes are shown in tables 2-1 and 2-2.

30. See table A-1 for comparative statistics.

Table 2-2. Enlistments of Female Recruits, Fiscal Years 1972–76
Numbers in thousands

Military Service	1972		1973		1974		1975		1976	
	Number	Percent of total recruits	Number	Percent of total recruits	Number	Percent of total recruits	Number	Percent of total recruits	Number	Percent of total recruits
Army	6.0	3.3	8.3	4.1	15.1	8.4	18.4	10.3	15.8	8.8
Navy	2.2	2.5	4.9	5.3	6.8	7.5	6.4	6.7	5.0	5.9
Marine Corps	0.7	1.3	0.7	1.4	0.9	1.9	1.3	2.3	1.4	2.4
Air Force	4.8	5.4	6.3	6.8	8.2	11.1	9.6	13.2	8.6	12.0
Department of Defense total	13.6	3.3	20.3	4.6	30.9	7.9	35.6	8.8	30.8	7.9

Source: Derived from unpublished data provided by the Assistant Secretary of Defense for Manpower and Reserve Affairs, October 1976.

Second, changes have been made in personnel policies, the most notable are:[31]

• Permitting women to command organizations composed of both men and women;

  • Allowing women to enter aviation training and military academies.

• Eliminating policies that require the automatic discharge of pregnant women and those with minor dependents.

• Equalizing family entitlements for married servicemen and service-women.

• Giving women access to a wider range of training opportunities (for example, Army women can be trained to use light antitank weapons, the M-16 rifle, the grenade launcher, the claymore mine, and the M-60 machine gun).

Third, apart from training, changes have taken place in the kinds of jobs to which women can be assigned. Traditionally, in peacetime, women in the military performed nursing or clerical duties; in fact, prior to the 1972 expansion, only 35 percent of all military enlisted job specialties were open to women. Following an initial reassessment in 1972, over 80 percent of the specialties were opened to women; and by 1976 they could be used in all but the combat-associated specialties.

Fourth, the proportion of women *actually* assigned to nontraditional jobs has increased. Less than 10 percent of all enlisted women were assigned to nontraditional jobs in 1972; by 1976 about 40 percent were assigned to scientific, technical, or blue-collar labor specialties. These changes are detailed in table 2-4.

Finally, the influx of women has also influenced the socioeconomic composition of the enlisted ranks. Table 2-3 presents a comparative profile of male and female recruits entering the armed forces from 1973 to 1976. The average woman recruit is about one year older, as likely to be married, but less likely to be black than her male counterpart. She surpasses the average male recruit in educational attainment and in the standardized tests—two yardsticks most frequently used by the armed forces to measure "quality." Under the dual standards of selection applied to male and female recruits, she is more apt, by far, to have a high school diploma and

31. A summary of changes in policies related to women can be found in Department of Defense, "Manpower Requirements Report for FY 1977" (DOD, February 1976; processed), chap. 16, and Department of Defense, "Manpower Requirements Report for FY 1978" (DOD, March 1977; processed), chap. 16.

Table 2-3. **Characteristics of Male and Female Recruits, by Service, Fiscal Years 1973–76**
Percent or years

Characteristic	Army Male	Army Female	Navy Male	Navy Female	Marine Corps Male	Marine Corps Female	Air Force Male	Air Force Female	Department of Defense total Male	Department of Defense total Female
Average age	19.1	20.2	18.6	19.8	18.5	19.3	19.1	20.0	18.9	20.0
Proportion married	14.0	14.0	6.1	4.4	5.2	1.4	17.1	13.7	11.6	11.6
Proportion black	23.9	19.0	10.4	10.1	19.9	16.2	14.0	15.3	18.5	16.1
Proportion with high school diplomas[a]	54.1	88.4	70.4	98.6	48.0	90.9	85.8	93.0	62.9	91.7
Average standardized test score[b]	51.8	73.2	58.2	52.9	56.1	66.7	62.3	62.7	55.8	66.0
Average duration of initial enlistment	3.0	3.0	4.0	3.8	3.5	3.2	4.3	4.3	3.5	3.5
Proportion in service at end of 1976	57.7	67.7	66.6	70.2	64.8	58.1	72.8	74.0	63.4	69.6

Source: Based on data provided by OASD, Manpower and Reserve Affairs, October 1976, and OASD, Manpower and Reserves Affairs, "Use of Women in the Military," p. 10.

a. Includes bona fide high school graduates only; those with General Educational Development (GED) test equivalency, who are sometimes counted for Department of Defense purposes, are not included here.

b. The standardized tests administered to recruits are discussed in chapter 7.

Table 2-4. Percentage Distribution of Female Enlisted Personnel
by Occupational Category, End of Fiscal Years 1972 and 1976

Occupational Category	1972	1976
Traditional	**90.6**	**59.9**
Medical and dental specialists	23.8	18.6
Administrative specialists and clerks	66.8	41.3
Nontraditional	**9.4**	**40.2**
Infantry, gun crew, and allied specialists	0.2	0.2
Electronic equipment repairmen	1.2	4.3
Communications and intelligence specialists	4.2	15.0
Other technical specialists	2.8	2.7
Electrical/mechanical equipment repairmen	0.0	6.7
Craftsmen	0.1	1.4
Service and supply handlers	0.9	9.9

Sources: Fiscal year 1972, Central All-Volunteer Task Force, "Utilization of Military Women" (OASD, Manpower and Reserve Affairs, December 1972; processed), p. 26; fiscal 1976 data provided by OASD, Manpower and Reserve Affairs, February 17, 1977.

she scored ten points higher on the standardized tests. And although enlistees of both sexes signed up for approximately the same average duration of service, men had a higher attrition rate and hence a larger proportion of women who enlisted during the period were still in the service at the end of 1976. In sum, over the 1972–76 period, women recruits raised the average quality of the armed forces; they tended to equalize the racial mix with that of the overall population; and, on average, served longer than their male counterparts. The implications of these differences are discussed in chapter 6.

Future Prospects

Given the present course, however, women's expanding participation in the armed forces is largely in the past. The high rate of increase that occurred during the first half of the seventies, averaging about 20 percent annually, started to abate in fiscal 1976. As table 2-5 shows, total annual growth is expected to average about 5 percent a year through fiscal 1982, at which time some 147,000 women will constitute about 7 percent of the armed forces.

The Army and Navy plan to concentrate future growth among women officers, whereas the number of enlisted women in both services will

Table 2-5. Actual and Projected Female Military Personnel Strengths, End of Fiscal Years 1976–82

Women in thousands

		Projected					
Military service and class	Actual 1976	1977	1978	1979	1980	1981	1982
Army	48.7	52.2	55.1	57.7	58.3	58.9	59.4
Officer	4.8	5.9	6.7	7.3	7.9	8.5	9.0
Enlisted	43.9	46.3	48.4	50.4	50.4	50.4	50.4
Navy	22.7	23.5	25.1	25.3	25.5	25.7	25.9
Officer	3.5	3.8	4.0	4.2	4.4	4.6	4.8
Enlisted	19.2	19.6	21.1	21.1	21.1	21.1	21.1
Marine Corps	3.4	3.9	4.2	5.1	5.8	6.3	7.3
Officer	0.3	0.4	0.5	0.5	0.5	0.6	0.6
Enlisted	3.1	3.5	3.7	4.6	5.3	5.8	6.7
Air Force	34.0	40.0	46.0	48.0	50.0	52.0	54.0
Officer	4.8	5.4	5.8	5.8	5.8	5.8	5.8
Enlisted	29.2	34.6	40.2	42.2	44.2	46.2	48.2
Department of Defense total	108.8	119.6	130.4	136.1	139.6	142.9	146.6
Officer	13.4	15.5	17.0	17.8	18.6	19.5	20.2
Enlisted	95.4	104.0	113.4	118.3	121.0	123.5	126.4
Total number of women as percent of total military personnel[a]	5.2	5.7	6.2	6.5	6.6	6.8	7.0

Sources: OASD, Manpower and Reserve Affairs, "Use of Women in the Military." Details may not add to totals because of rounding.

a. Assumes a total military strength of 2.1 million throughout the period.

stabilize.[32] The Marine Corps and Air Force, on the other hand, plan increases in enlisted women while their female officer corps are projected to remain at a fairly constant level.[33]

Beyond the question of numbers and roles several practices that discriminate against military women remain in effect. Since the demand for female recruits is smaller than it is for males, the services have set educa-

32. Office of the Assistant Secretary of Defense for Manpower and Reserve Affairs, "Use of Women in the Military," background study (OASD, Manpower and Reserve Affairs, May 1977; processed), pp. 32, 40. The Navy goal of 21,000 enlisted women represents the "current approved plan." Apparently the Navy is considering an alternative that would increase that goal to about 30,000 by fiscal 1983.

33. Ibid., pp. 44, 47. It should be noted that Air Force figures are tentative. Officially, Air Force planning with respect to the number of women extends only through fiscal 1978. According to the Air Force, "we have not yet established the plan to be effected at the beginning of FY 1979. We have, however, done extensive work toward the development of the plan we hope to implement" (ibid., p. C-9).

tional, intelligence, aptitude, and physical standards for women that may be in excess of those necessary for the satisfactory performance of many duties to which they are assigned. Also, the status of dependent children remains an obstacle to enlistment for certain women, but not for their male counterparts. Given the progress to date, it is likely that these issues —along with a host of other distinctions in the conditions of service between men and women—will be addressed regardless of any decision to increase the role of women.

CHAPTER THREE

CURRENT POLICIES
AND THEIR IMPLICATIONS

Despite recent progress in opening up job opportunities for women, the military establishment nonetheless remains predominantly a male organization. Women are not at present intended to constitute more than 7 percent of total strength. Current policies in the armed forces that limit women's programs in each of the services are discussed below before an examination of the arguments for and against further expansion of the role of women in the chapters to follow.

Air Force

Statutory provisions embodied in the Women's Armed Services Integration Act of 1948 provide for the following:

The Secretary of the Air Force shall prescribe the military authority which female persons of the Air Force may exercise, and the kind of military duty to which they may be assigned: *Provided,* That they shall not be assigned to duty in aircraft while such aircraft are engaged in combat missions.[1]

Thus the Air Force was given wide latitude in constructing policies governing the type of work available to women. In its imprecision, the law left much open to interpretation. Though the term "combat" was never well defined, the Air Force selected the most rigid definition and until recently barred women from serving as crewmembers aboard any aircraft, regardless of mission and, hence, from any job (such as training and supervisory positions) for which crewmember experience is considered a prerequisite.[2] Since Air Force policy further excludes women from duties involving "combat operations by actually engaging the enemy and/or

1. Women's Armed Services Integration Act of 1948, 62 Stat. 373.
2. Women could be assigned as non-crewmembers; for example, women have served as flight nurses and flight attendants. In 1975, the Air Force established a test program to train a small number of women as pilots and navigators for duty aboard

delivering weapons upon the enemy,"[3] duties involving the operation of land-based missiles have also been closed to them. Based on these restrictions, women cannot be assigned to about 30,000 officer billets.[4]

In addition, the number of men trained as pilots and navigators must exceed the number of positions for these skills. This surplus ensures that pilots and navigators will not have to remain on flight duty continuously and also provides a mobilization base for wartime. In fiscal 1977, about 6,500 behind-the-line jobs for which women might otherwise be qualified, are being reserved for male pilots and navigators.[5] In fact, jobs closed to women officers number about 36,000 or about 40 percent of the total.

The jobs open to enlisted women in the Air Force are far less restricted. Of fifty-seven enlisted occupational fields, all but eleven can be filled by women. The closed specialties are air crewmember, aerial gunner, inflight refueling operator, flight engineer, aircraft loadmaster, member of pararescue recovery team, member of combat control team, ground radio communications equipment repairman (parachutist), missile system maintenance specialist, missile facilities specialist, and security specialist. Altogether, only 31,000 jobs, or about 6 percent, are closed to Air Force enlisted women for "combat" reasons.[6]

In addition to this occupational constraint, moreover, an additional 83,000 assignments are closed because of housing limitations, mostly at overseas locations. According to the Air Force, lack of adequate facilities for unmarried women precluded them from being assigned to about 45 percent of all jobs located overseas.

"support" aircraft. See Office of the Assistant Secretary of Defense for Manpower and Reserve Affairs, "Use of Women in the Military," background study (OASD, Manpower and Reserve Affairs, May 1977; processed), p. 42. Note: page references throughout this text are from a preliminary version of this study.

3. United States Air Force, *Air Force Regulation 35-30*.

4. Based on data provided by the deputy director, Personnel Plans for Human Resources Development, U.S. Air Force, September 7, 1976.

5. Reported in *Air Force Times* (November 22, 1976), p. 12.

6. Information on the Air Force program is from OASD, Manpower and Reserve Affairs, "Use of Women in the Military," pp. 41–45. The figures in this analysis, unlike those presented in the OASD study, have been adjusted for "pipeline" personnel. That is, in addition to the actual jobs to be done, the military services also maintain a pool of people to offset those absent from their jobs while traveling between assignments, attending schools, and the like. These extra personnel ostensibly are used to keep units at full strength. For example, to keep 415,000 enlisted jobs filled in fiscal 1977, the Air Force had an average of 477,000 people assigned. Throughout this analysis, it is assumed that these pipeline requirements are distributed proportionately to enlisted jobs.

The remaining 363,000 Air Force jobs (76 percent of the total) could conceivably be filled by qualified men *or* women within currently prescribed Air Force policy; yet, according to current plans, only about one in every eight are to be filled by a woman by fiscal 1982. It can only be concluded that either the Air Force is unable to attract enough qualified women or that the sex composition of the Air Force is shaped largely by the Air Force's preference to remain a predominantly male institution and by its ability to attract a sufficient number of qualified males.

Navy

As in the case of the Air Force, Congress in 1948 placed specific limitations on how the Navy could utilize its women personnel:

The Secretary of the Navy may prescribe the manner in which women shall be trained and qualified for military duty in the Regular Navy, the military authority which they may exercise, and the kind of military duty to which they may be assigned: *Provided,* That they shall not be assigned to duty in aircraft while such aircraft are engaged in combat missions nor shall they be assigned to duty on vessels of the Navy except hospital ships and naval transports.[7]

Since there are currently no hospital or transport vessels in the fleet, all seagoing jobs are closed to women.[8]

In addition, the Navy precludes the assignment of women to some land-based units (for example, antisubmarine warfare squadrons), which operate away from their home base for extensive periods. Because of these

7. Women's Armed Services Integration Act of 1948, 62 Stat. 368. In April 1977, however, the Navy submitted to Congress a proposal to alter the law to give the secretary of the Navy greater leeway in assigning women aboard naval vessels. The proposal uses the following language: "However, women may not be assigned to duty in vessels or aircraft that are engaged in combat missions nor may they be assigned to other than temporary duty on vessels of the Navy except for hospital ships, transports, and vessels of a similar classification not expected to be assigned combat missions." If approved by Congress, this change is expected to make possible the assignment of women to certain auxiliary and support ships and certain aviation squadrons. The roster of vessels and squadrons that would be affected had not been announced by May 1977. (Department of Defense legislative proposal, DOD 95-75, "To amend section 6015 of title 10, United States Code, to permit the Secretary of the Navy to prescribe the kind of military duty to which women members of the naval service may be assigned.")

8. By the Navy's interpretation, women may be assigned to small harbor craft and tugboats as long as they do not deploy to the high seas; in early 1976 about 300 women were assigned on these vessels. See "Women in Navy: As Numbers Increase, New Problems Arise," *Navy Times* (March 29, 1976), p. 15.

Table 3-1. Maximum Number of Women Assignable to Yeoman Rating

Rank	Sea-duty billets (1)	Unrestricted billets (2)	Maximum number of billets assignable to women[a] (3)
E-7, E-8, E-9	589	906	317
E-5, E-6	1,200	3,023	1,823
E-4 and below	2,115	1,972	-143
Total	3,904	5,901	1,997

Source: Data provided by the Department of the Navy, March 1977.
a. Column 2 minus column 1.

restrictions, of a total of 464,000 Navy enlisted billets, about 287,000 (62 percent) are closed to women.[9]

This is not to say, however, that the remaining 177,000 enlisted billets could be filled by women. The Navy must have more personnel qualified for sea duty than they have seagoing jobs. For example, if women were permitted to fill a large number of shore-based positions, fewer men could be assigned ashore and they would have to spend a longer time at sea. To guard against this, a minimum number of shore billets are set aside for men to ensure that one is available for every sailor returning from a pre-scribed sea tour. This computation is made for each occupational area.

To illustrate, table 3-1 shows that in the aggregate women can occupy 1,997 of a total of 9,805 billets in the yeoman occupational specialty with-out disrupting the sea-shore rotation pattern for men. However, when there are more sea-duty than shore-duty billets in the "E-4 and below" group, as there are in this rating, adjustments are necessary. The recom-mended number of women employed is the smaller of (a) twice the assign-able jobs in grades E-5 and E-6 or (b) 80 percent of the unrestricted bil-lets to which women can be assigned in grades E-4 and below. This method of assignment, which according to the Navy is to ensure that men would not have to serve a disproportionate share of their time at sea, yields a maximum goal of 1,577 women (80 percent of 1,972) in the yeoman rating.[10]

After applying this methodology to all ratings, and based on a rotation pattern of thirty-six months at sea and an equal time ashore, the Navy

9. "Use of Women in the Military," p. 38, adjusted for pipeline. In fiscal 1977 the Navy had an average of 464,000 enlisted people to keep 382,000 jobs filled.
10. Estimates provided by the Department of the Navy, March 1977. It should be pointed out that a sea tour does not involve continuous deployment afloat. Over a three-year sea tour, for example, a sailor may spend about one-third of his time afloat—an average of one year at sea.

estimates that a total of 22,362 enlisted women could be employed without adversely affecting male sea-shore rotation patterns. According to the Navy, however, further adjustments necessitated by berthing constraints and mobilization considerations reduce the total to about 20,000, or 4.3 percent of total Navy enlisted strength.[11] Allowing for the pipeline, the figure becomes 24,000.

By a basically similar method the Navy has set a goal for women officers of 2,000 by 1985 in what is termed the "unrestricted line"—the category of women officers who are not assigned to one of the "staff corps" (for example, nurses or supply corps) or to the "restricted line," which includes such specialties as engineering duty, public affairs, cryptology, and the like. All of the staff corps have been open to women since the early 1970s and generally quantitative limits have not been imposed. The "restricted line" communities were opened to women in April 1976 and goals for those categories of jobs are still being evaluated. For planning purposes, the Navy has projected a total goal of about 5,000 women officers, to be achieved by 1983.[12]

Army

Restrictions on the utilization of women in the Army are conspicuously absent from the statutory provisions of the 1948 act, which simply states: "The Secretary of the Army shall prescribe the military authority which commissioned officers of the Women's Army Corps may exercise, and the kind of military duty to which they may be assigned" (62 Stat. 359). The Army preferred to have specific combat restrictions excluded at that time for reasons explained by the director of the Women's Army Corps:

While it is War Department policy to limit the utilization of women in the Army to noncombat jobs, it is impossible for the War Department to outline combat areas in the future since the experts advise that modern warfare makes the entire United States vulnerable as a combat area in the future.[13]

11. Ibid. It appears, however, that the Navy is in the midst of reassessing its methodology and revising upward its estimate of the number of jobs open to women. Though not approved by May 1977, the Navy had unveiled a plan to open about 30,000 jobs to enlisted women by 1982. (See OASD, Manpower and Reserve Affairs, "Use of Women in the Military," pp. 38–40.)

12. Ibid.

13. "Testimony by Colonel Mary Hallaren," *Women's Armed Services Integration Act of 1947,* Hearings before the Senate Armed Services Committee, 80:1 (GPO, 1947), p. 88.

Although the law was imprecise, ambiguous, and incomplete, the Army had little doubt that Congress opposed the assignment of women to jobs that would expose them to danger or to duties considered physically too arduous. It is this interpretation upon which are based the premises underlying Army policies concerning the employment of women: first, the primary mission of the Army is combat and, second, this nation does not support the use of women in direct combat roles.

Through the years, however, the Army has altered its views of what constitutes a direct combat role. Before the recent pressure to expand, only 185 of the Army's 482 enlisted job specialties were open to women.[14] Even more restrictive, however, was the policy precluding the assignment of women to units whose mission was related to combat or combat support, which meant that women could only be assigned to about one-third of all Army units. Even in those units, however, only 19,000 enlisted jobs were considered "interchangeable"; that is, they could be filled by either men or women. At that time, about 12,300 enlisted women were assigned to these units.[15]

In 1972, with the approval of a plan to double the number of women in the Army, all except forty-eight specialties were opened to women, the restrictions against assignment to combat-related units were modified, and a goal of 50,000 enlisted Army women was announced. As matters stood in May 1977, women were excluded from thirty-one combat skills and from units whose primary mission includes engaging and inflicting casualties or equipment damage on the enemy and that typically operate forward of the brigade rear boundary. The job breakdown is shown below:

	Restricted jobs	*Unrestricted jobs*	*Total number of jobs*
Jobs in male-only units	149,000	112,000	261,000
Jobs in unrestricted units	20,000	286,000	306,000
Total number of jobs	169,000	398,000	567,000

Of the total 567,000 jobs for enlisted personnel, 281,000 are closed to women—261,000 in restricted (male-only) units and an additional 20,000, which although they are not in restricted units are nevertheless in restricted skills.

14. Department of the Army, Office of the Deputy Chief of Personnel, "Women in the Army Study" (Department of the Army, December 1976; processed), pp. 5-2, 5-3.

15. Information on enlisted jobs are from data provided by the Department of the Army, April 1977.

The remaining 286,000 positions involving unrestricted jobs in unrestricted units are, in Army terminology, "interchangeable"; that is, they could conceivably be filled by men or women.

Women cannot be assigned to all interchangeable jobs, however. The Army desires that fixed proportions be assigned to different types of units depending on the proximity of those units to combat action. The closer to the forward edge of the battle area (FEBA) that a unit habitually operates, so the logic goes, the lower the proportion of women that should be assigned. According to the Army, forward-based personnel are more apt to engage in direct combat and units located in the battle sector are likely to move more often, thus placing greater physical demands on its personnel.

In general, the proportions of women are limited in the following manner:

1. No more than 10 percent of the personnel in units serving in the division area, between brigade and division rear boundaries—typically situated between 30 and 50 kilometers from the FEBA.

2. No more than 15 to 30 percent (depending on the type of unit) of units operating between division and corps rear boundaries, typically between 50 and 150 kilometers from the FEBA.

3. No more than 25 to 45 percent (depending on the type of unit) of units operating behind the corps area.

4. Up to 50 percent of the personnel in units assigned in the continental United States that are not expected to deploy overseas.[16]

Finally to take into account personnel management considerations, the Army sets aside a number of additional jobs for men that would otherwise be open to women to ensure that the men are provided equitable promotion and assignment opportunities.[17]

Together these restrictions limit to about 45,000 the number of jobs open to Army enlisted women, a figure that is raised to about 55,000 after allowance is made for the pipeline (see table 3-2). The Army, nonetheless, has not altered its goal of 50,400 enlisted women that was established in

16. Department of the Army, "Women in the Army Study," pp. 5-8, 5-9.

17. The Army employs a series of computer models to calculate the effects of various management decisions. The Women's Enlisted Expansion Model (WEEM) takes promotion, rotation, and other factors into account. The Enlisted Force Management Plan (EFMP) calculates a maximum number of women recruits per year based on desired grade distributions and expected reenlistment rates. For discussion of the models, see ibid., chaps. 3 and 5.

Table 3-2. Projected Number of Army Enlisted Jobs Open to Women
Thousands

Type of enlisted jobs	Positions available to women
Total (including pipeline)	**676**
Less jobs closed to women	415
All jobs in combat units	261
Combat jobs in noncombat units	20
Geographical guidelines	68
Pipeline allowance	66
Less jobs reserved for men	206
Rotation base requirements	23
Career development	150
Pipeline allowance	33
Total number of enlisted jobs open to women	**55**

Source: Office of the Assistant Secretary for Manpower and Reserve Affairs, "Use of Women in the Military," background study (OASD, Manpower and Reserve Affairs, May 1977), pp. 31-32, adjusted for pipeline allowances. In fiscal 1977, the Army needed an average of 676,000 enlisted personnel to keep 567,000 jobs filled. It should be noted that the number of jobs indicated as closed to women by the geographical guidelines—68,000—does not represent the actual number of positions that are affected by the guidelines. Altogether there are about 130,000 jobs in that category, but about 60,000 of them would be closed to women in any event because of career development considerations.

1972. A similar analysis indicates that the Army could accommodate about 9,000 women officers (including nurses), a goal not expected to be reached before 1982.[18]

Marine Corps

Limitations on the recruitment of women in the Marine Corps, while not established by law, are indirectly influenced by the prohibition against women serving aboard naval vessels. Since the primary mission of the Corps is amphibious warfare, the bulk of Marine units deploy periodically aboard amphibious ships. In fact, about 99,000, or 72 percent of all enlisted billets, are in combat divisions, aircraft wings, force troops, and force service regiments, which collectively compose the Fleet Marine Forces. Of this total, about 500 in the rear echelon, which according to the Marine Corps would not be required to deploy with the assault forces in an emergency, have been opened to women.

With respect to occupational opportunities, all but four fields have been opened to women marines: infantry, field artillery, tank and amphibian tractor crew, and aircrew. These limitations close to women an additional

18. Ibid., p. 32.

1,300 jobs that, while not in Fleet Marine Force units, nevertheless require these skills.

Of the remaining enlisted positions, the Marine Corps has set aside about 28,400 as a rotation base and another 2,400 to maintain grade structure and allow for promotion flow. Thus, all told, about 6,900 enlisted jobs are open to women marines; to keep these jobs filled, the Corps would require about 8,500 women. Nonetheless, the Marine Corps plans to have 6,700 women by fiscal 1982. Based on similar logic, a maximum of about 600 women officers by 1982 is envisaged.[19]

CONTRARY TO WIDELY HELD BELIEFS, the major restrictions on the recruitment and functions assigned to women in the United States military establishment are not explicitly incorporated in federal law. To be sure, few opportunities in either the Army or Air Force would be closed to women if the statutory provisions governing the utilization of military women were literally interpreted. More limiting are the set of policies established by the military services themselves based on their own interpretations of the national will as expressed through Congress. Together, these laws and policies relegate women to a minor role.

Whether or not these laws and policies should be changed and, if so, how they should be changed are the questions addressed in the following chapters.

19. Ibid., pp. 46–48, D-1 to D-4.

CHAPTER FOUR

<hr>

WOMEN'S RIGHTS
AND MILITARY BENEFITS

Equality between the sexes ranks high on the agenda of this nation's social issues. Closely tied to the impact that the women's movement has had on the family and the economy—indeed on virtually every segment of society—has been its effects on the military establishment. In some respects, the armed forces are ahead of other national institutions in removing discriminatory practices and in tearing down traditional barriers. Yet, after several years of rapid evolution, the pace of change has slowed and the number and role of women in the armed forces are now circumscribed by the laws and policies discussed in the previous chapter.

Increasingly, the propriety of these laws and policies is being questioned. Proponents of women's rights argue that because of the discriminatory aspects of existing provisions, qualified females are not permitted to compete with men on an equal basis and, hence, women are being excluded from equally sharing a variety of economic and social benefits.

While these charges are generally levied by feminists against most American institutions, the military establishment is singled out because (1) with over two million jobs, it employs more people than any other government agency or any private company; (2) many feel that the institution established to protect and defend the nation should be a model of enlightenment and egalitarianism; and (3) the military provides a range of opportunities not readily available, particularly to women, in the private sector. These opportunities, some of which are unique to military service, are described below.

Economic Opportunities

More than 400,000 young people enter the armed services each year and attain an economic status that many of them would find difficult to

31

Figure 4-1. Comparison of Mean Annual Earnings of Civilians with College Education, by Sex and Age, and Commissioned Officers, by Age, 1975[a]

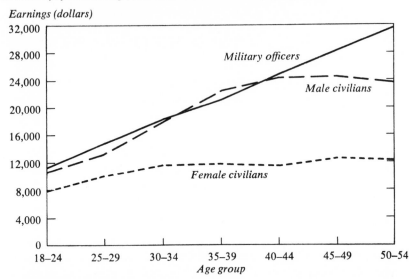

Sources: Military earnings—basic pay, quarters and subsistence allowance, and the tax advantages that accrue because allowances are not taxable—based on unpublished data provided by the Office of the Assistant Secretary of Defense for Manpower and Reserve Affairs, October 1976; civilian earnings based on unpublished data provided by the U.S. Department of Commerce, Bureau of the Census, November 1976.

a. Civilians employed full time with four or more years of college. It should be noted that too much emphasis should not be attached to the divergence beyond the 40–44 age group in annual earnings between military officers and male civilians. There are relatively few military officers beyond that age group and they are generally in high-ranking positions analogous to executives in the private sector.

Figure 4-2. Comparison of Mean Annual Earnings of Civilians by Sex and Age, and Military Enlisted Personnel, by Age, 1975[a]

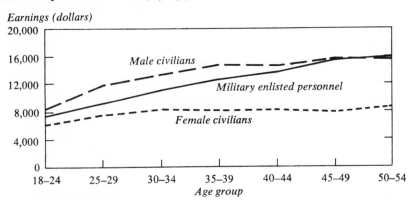

Sources: Same as figure 1.

a. Civilians employed full time with at least four years of high school but less than four years of college.

duplicate in the private sector. In addition to an attractive compensation package consisting of pay, allowances, and a variety of benefits, a wide range of education and training programs are available.

Military Pay

Since the end of the military draft, a recruitment system based on market forces has replaced a system in which heavy reliance on conscription resulted in underpayment of military personnel. To keep pace with this change, military pay has been increased and by most accounts has not only reached comparability with federal civilian pay, but now appears to be sufficiently competitive to attract the necessary number of volunteers from the civilian labor force.[1] Some would argue, however, that a sufficient quantity of recruits is being attracted at present pay levels only at the expense of quality. This issue is discussed in chapter 6.

The relative attractiveness of military pay scales is illustrated in figures 1 and 2. Figure 1 compares average annual earnings of military officers in 1975 with those of civilians in the same age group who had completed at least four years of college and were employed full time. The differences between the earnings of male civilians and military officers, on the one hand, and female civilians on the other, are prominent. A similar, but less pronounced difference appears in figure 2, which compares military enlisted personnel with civilians in the same age group who had completed high school but had not completed college. However, both cases illustrate why military pay scales, *which are the same regardless of sex,* are relatively more attractive to women than to men.

Supplementing pay and allowances are a variety of nonpecuniary benefits the most important of which are retirement and medical care.

RETIREMENT. By far the most valuable fringe benefit available to military personnel is the military retirement program. When retirement annuities become vested, after twenty years of service, retirees are entitled to 50 percent of their terminal basic pay. Annuities are increased at the rate of 2.5 percent of basic pay for each year beyond twenty years to a maximum of 75 percent. In addition, those found physically unfit for further service are granted physical disability retirements, with the nature

1. As used here, military earnings include basic pay, quarters and subsistence allowances, and the tax advantage that accrues because allowances are not taxable. Together these elements constitute Regular Military Compensation, which is taken to be the military equivalent of a civilian salary.

and amount of benefits dependent on the degree of disability. Since the system is noncontributory and not funded, it is difficult to express the benefit in terms of current military compensation. Retirement is of no value to a person who does not serve long enough to acquire vested rights but among those who do the accrued annual value could range from 50 to over 100 percent of basic pay, depending on rank, age at retirement, and assumptions concerning future pay and price increases. The typical retiree can expect to collect more total pay during retirement than he or she collected during active service. Hence, those who select a military career are provided a level of financial security that few men and even fewer women would be able to match in the civilian sector.

MEDICAL CARE. Military personnel on active duty are also entitled to unlimited health care. Their dependents receive medical care in military facilities, subject to availability. The rates are adjusted periodically. There is no charge for outpatient care, but when hospitalized, dependents of active-duty military personnel are charged (as of May 1977) at the rate of $4.10 a day. When military facilities are not available, dependent spouses and children are entitled to use civilian facilities. For inpatient services, the government pays all expenses except for a charge of $4.10 a day or $25, whichever is greater. For outpatient care, the sponsor pays the first $50 a year for each dependent, or the first $100 a year for a family with two or more dependents. Beyond that, the government pays 80 percent of the bill. Similar, but less liberal, formulas are applied to health services provided for retirees and their dependents. And in some cases, veterans with only a few years of active military service can qualify for medical care in Veterans Administration facilities after leaving the armed forces, whether or not the medical condition was service-connected.

OTHER BENEFITS. Some benefits, such as social security, unemployment compensation, leave benefits, and separation pay, are also available to civilian employees in the private sector. However, others such as commissaries and exchanges, low-cost insurance, veterans' bonuses, veterans' loans, veterans' preference in federal and state employment, extra points on civil service tests, and less likelihood of losing government jobs during work reductions are not.

EVALUATION OF "TOTAL" EARNINGS. Because of the inherent complexity of the compensation system and the problems in evaluating its elements, it is difficult to obtain agreement on the magnitude of "total" military earnings. By conservative estimates, however, the value of fringe benefits considered unique to military service increases military "salaries" on average by at least 25 percent.[2] When the value of these benefits is included in the calculations, the relative economic attractiveness of a military career, especially to women, is further underscored.

Caution must be exercised, however, in interpreting these results. The attractiveness of the military pay package must be measured in light of the burdens. Many risks, deprivations, inconveniences, and hardships are also unique to military life. However, these burdens are neither uniformly distributed among all military personnel nor do they appear closely related to the military compensation system.

The plight of many lower-grade enlisted personnel, some with dependents who are required to pay the expenses of moving their families and household goods, some who work inordinately long hours, some who may endure forced family separation, and some who may be subject to middle-of-the-night surprise inspections, has few counterparts in the private sector. The advantages enjoyed by many higher-ranking career personnel, on the other hand, who are able to keep regular hours in a variety of technical and administrative jobs, who are often furnished family quarters at far less than fair market rates, and who are disproportionately rewarded by the benefit structure, also have few nonmilitary counterparts. These are extremely emotional and misunderstood issues, a full discussion of which is beyond the scope of this paper.[3] It is enough to point out that the military pay system, racked with inequities and inefficiencies, is in need of reform. Nonetheless, the conclusions reached in this chapter regarding the benefits accruing to the average military person under the present compensation system appear reasonable. Moreover, even if the military pay estimates depicted in figures 1 and 2 are considered to have an upward bias, that bias would have to be significant in order to offset the obvious attraction of military pay to women.

Job Training and Educational Assistance

As the nation's largest single vocational training institution, each year the armed services offer to thousands of people an opportunity to acquire skills and knowledge that not only enable them to carry out their military duties but, in many instances, prepare them for more productive careers when they leave the service. In fiscal 1977, for example, over 400,000

2. Described in Martin Binkin, *The Military Pay Muddle* (Brookings Institution, 1975), pp. 28–29.
3. For a more extensive discussion of these problems, see ibid.

recruits are expected to enter about 625 different initial-skill training courses, some 160,000 of whom will eventually take advanced courses.[4] These courses encompass a wide range of occupations; some, such as training for the combat arms, have little transferability to civilian life, while others, such as law enforcement and mechanical and electronics training, make military service a path to a productive civilian career.

By virtue of their active service, military personnel are also provided with a broad range of educational opportunities. Chief among these is the educational assistance provided by the GI Bill, ranging from college courses to vocational and on-the-job training. Under the Veterans' Readjustment Benefits Act of 1966[5] eligible veterans who enlisted before January 1, 1977, are entitled to assistance for a period of one and one-half months (or the equivalent in part-time training) for each month of service on active duty. The maximum period of training depends on a variety of factors, but in no case can it exceed forty-eight months. Effective October 1, 1976, monthly payments for those in full-time programs are $292 for a single veteran, $347 for a married veteran, $396 for a married veteran with a child, and $24 for each additional dependent.[6] Tuition, books, fees, and other educational expenses are paid for by the beneficiary. Low-interest loans of up to $1,500 yearly are also made available; repayments are not due until nine months after the borrower ceases to be a student and can be made over a period of ten years. Eligible individuals have ten years after separation, or until December 31, 1989, whichever is earlier, to complete the program.[7]

Persons signing enlistment contracts after January 1, 1977, are covered under the Veterans' Education and Employment Assistance Act of 1976.[8] Under the provisions of this law, which depart from the grant system operating under the previous act, a voluntary contributory educational assistance program will give service personnel an opportunity to contribute $50 or $75 monthly, up to a maximum of $2,700, toward their future education. The government will match the participants' contribu-

4. Department of Defense, "Military Manpower Training Report for FY 1977" (DOD, March 1976; processed), chap. 5.
5. 80 Stat. 12-28. Although the act is widely known as the Vietnam Era GI Bill, its only explicitly declared purposes were to encourage enlistment and to compensate former military men and women for the "disruption" of their careers caused by military service. Its benefits were extended to all who had served since the end of the Korean War.
6. 38 U.S.C., sec. 1682 as amended, and 90 Stat. 2385.
7. 38 U.S.C., sec. 1798 as amended, and 90 Stat. 2399.
8. 90 Stat. 2383-406.

tions by two to one. Furthermore, the Pentagon has been given the authority to contribute even greater amounts as enlistment incentives.

A variety of educational programs are also available to military people while they are still on active duty. For example, under a tuition assistance program, the government will pay up to 75 percent of the tuition and expenses for off-duty courses at civilian educational institutions regardless of how long the military personnel have served.[9]

In sum, the armed forces provide opportunities for job training and educational assistance not elsewhere available, particularly to disadvantaged youth. Countless male high school dropouts have entered the military, earned diplomas, learned marketable skills, and returned to civilian life as more productive members of society. The inequities are highlighted by one observer:

> Women are denied the opportunity to obtain the job training and experience available to servicemen from working class and minority group backgrounds. It is well known that the armed services serve as a "college" for many of the nation's poor; I fail to see why women should be deprived of this opportunity.[10]

Social Opportunities

The basic social context in which military people exist is strikingly important. They deal with, work with, and befriend others with diverse life styles and aspirations. They recognize a larger world and the disciplinary process indispensable to success in that world. They assimilate new values and learn how to adhere to the rules imposed by the military. These attitudinal changes are often crucial to success in other institutions in American society. The extent to which women are judged on their abilities and performance rather than upon sexual differences could lead "to a higher estimation of their personal worth and to placing a higher value upon achievement and competence."[11]

Those who select the military as a career and rise through the ranks are also often able to achieve a social status far superior to many of their

9. Department of Defense Directive No. 1322.7, "Financial Assistance for Voluntary Educational Programs" (DOD, August 5, 1970; processed), and 90 Stat. 2395.

10. "Statement by Professor Norman Dorsen," *Equal Rights 1970,* Hearings before the Senate Judiciary Committee, 91:2 (GPO, 1970), p. 325.

11. Mariclaire Hale and Leo Kanowitz, "Women and the Draft: A Response to Critics of the Equal Rights Amendment," *The Hastings Law Journal,* vol. 23 (1971–72), p. 208.

civilian peers, particularly if they are disadvantaged members of minority groups. Even those who enlist for one tour are able to improve their educational credentials and acquire individual abilities that can help to improve their economic and social standing in civilian life.

It is also contended that because the military institution provides citizenship training with emphasis on voting, more women might become politically involved. To the extent that egalitarian principles govern social and economic relationships among military men and women, it is conceivable that upon completion of military service, women might be more inclined to participate in the political process. According to one commentator:

> The social stereotype is that women should be less concerned with the affairs of the world than men. Our political choices and our political debate often reflect a belief that men who have fought for their country have a special qualification or right to wield political power and make political decisions. Women are in no position to meet this qualification.[12]

Some have also argued that by being extended equal access to the military, women would have a viable alternative to the limited choice that still confronts many of them: higher education or marriage. Women not interested in college—or too poor to consider it—"may find themselves in the position where marriage seems the only possible salvation from drudgery and poverty. Poor and minority group women may be marrying during their teenage years because they see no realistic alternatives."[13] Teenage marriages account for the highest divorce rates and often involve children. In many cases, the mothers are left with the responsibility for the children and no means of support: "This type of poverty, in families headed by women, is perhaps the most difficult kind to cure."[14] Equal access to the armed forces could serve to interrupt that cycle by providing a period for maturing and reappraising responsibilities while upgrading skill attainment, job knowledge, and economic independence.

THUS, FROM THE INDIVIDUAL WOMAN'S PERSPECTIVE, the unique opportunities provided by the armed forces demand that present laws and policies be reassessed to determine whether remaining sex distinctions are justified by valid national security concerns or instead are anchored in sexual stereotypes of an earlier era.

12. "Statement by Professor Norman Dorsen," Hearings, p. 326.
13. Hale and Kanowitz, "Women and the Draft," p. 211.
14. Ibid.

CHAPTER FIVE

INSTITUTIONAL ATTITUDES

Women's role in the armed forces will ultimately depend on the extent to which national institutions—social, political, judicial, and military—are willing to break with their past—a past reflecting a persistent pattern of male dominance.

Public Opinion

The general public's view of the propriety of women in the armed forces is difficult to pin down. Despite its far-reaching social and military implications, there has been surprisingly little public discussion on the subject. No major national polls have directly addressed the question although several surveys have examined related issues.

A Roper Poll on women's rights conducted in 1971, "To Determine the Effects of Women's Liberation on the Thinking of Americans," asked for views on the statement: "Women should have equal treatment regarding the draft." Twenty-four percent of all respondents agreed, 71 percent disagreed, and the rest "didn't know."[1]

The lukewarm attitude of young civilian women in the early seventies is indicated in a survey commissioned by the Army in 1972. Asked to "rate their degree of favorability toward women's military service," 65 percent reported unfavorably (18 percent somewhat unfavorably and 47 percent very unfavorably) whereas only 17 percent regarded such a career with favor.[2]

1. Cited in *Congressional Record*, vol. 118, pt. 7 (1972), pp. 9099–100.
2. N. W. Ayer and Son, Inc., "A Study of Attitudes toward Enlistment in the Women's Army Corps" (March 1972; processed). When asked to estimate the atti-

A more limited 1973 survey, done in the Detroit area by the University of Michigan, measured attitudes toward the statement: "If anyone should bear arms, it should be men rather than women." Three-fourths of all respondents either "agreed" or "strongly agreed."[3]

A 1976 Gallup poll on perceptions of the role of women in society provides a more recent gauge of public thinking. Concerning the use of women in nontraditional jobs, respondents were asked to identify in which of nineteen occupations or professions "women would be better than men," and vice versa. The results, shown in table 5-1, indicate that stereotyped patterns persist: women are thought to be better suited for nursing, secretarial work, hairdressing, and teaching; men are considered to be better police officers, firemen, truck drivers, auto repairmen, and the like. Neither sex nor educational background radically affect opinions.[4]

In response to another question: "If you were taking a new job and had your choice of a boss, would you prefer to work for a man or for a woman?" only 7 percent of all respondents indicate they would prefer to work for a woman. Only 10 percent of the women would rather work for a woman.[5]

Recent setbacks to the Equal Rights Amendment carry at least some implication that the American public may not be ready to embrace the concept of full integration of women in the military establishment. Needing ratification by thirty-eight states to be enacted, the first twenty-two state legislatures ratified in 1973, three in 1974, one in 1975, and one in January 1977. The loss of the earlier momentum has been blamed in part on fears that the amendment would make women liable for military service. According to one commentator:

Opposition to the Amendment stems largely from those who fear that such a blanket prohibition on the use of sex as a legal classification will undermine traditional facets of the American culture, especially military and family law "protective" of women without achieving commensurate benefits.[6]

---

tudes of "young girls like themselves" to the same question, 39 percent reported unfavorably, while 33 percent responded favorably.

3. David R. Segal and others, "The Concept of Citizenship and Attitudes toward Women in Combat" (paper presented at the Fifth Symposium on Psychology in the Air Force, United States Air Force Academy, Colorado Springs, Colorado, April 8–10, 1976).

4. "Women in America," *Gallup Opinion Index,* Report No. 128 (March 1976).

5. Ibid.

6. Joan M. Krauskopf, "The Equal Rights Amendment: Its Political and Practical Contexts," *California State Bar Journal,* vol. 50 (March–April 1975), p. 136.

Table 5-1. Public Perceptions of the Role of Women in American Society,
Gallup Poll, 1976

	Percent of those polled who considered					
	Women to be better than men			Men to be better than women		
Occupation	Total	Male	Female	Total	Male	Female
Police officer	3	2	3	61	64	58
Doctor	14	12	17	31	33	29
Lawyer	8	7	9	34	37	32
Banker	8	8	7	29	31	28
Nurse	62	66	60	1	1	1
Auto mechanic	1	1	2	55	58	52
Stockbroker	5	5	5	27	28	27
Airline pilot	2	1	3	47	50	45
Truckdriver	2	2	2	56	58	54
Coalminer	a.	a.	a.	37	38	37
Executive of large corporation	7	4	9	32	35	29
U.S. senator	11	8	14	29	31	27
Elementary grade school teacher	52	56	50	4	4	4
Astronaut	2	1	2	44	44	44
Secretary	54	57	53	2	3	1
Fireman	a.	a.	1	56	58	55
Hairdresser	48	53	43	4	2	5
Veterinarian	14	16	13	25	25	26
Judge	16	12	19	29	32	27
All occupations	1	a.	2	10	11	9
No occupations	9	7	11	7	6	8
No opinion	15	16	14	5	5	6

Source: "Women in America," *Gallup Opinion Index*, Report No. 128 (March 1976), pp. 36–39.
a. Less than 1 percent.

Congressional Attitudes

Beyond national surveys, measures of public opinion are conveyed indirectly through elected officials. It appears that there is little opposition within Congress, at least in principle, to women serving in the military ranks. But how far this support would extend is difficult to discern. Would Congress, for example, accept an unlimited role for women—including combat assignments? The signals are mixed.

That Congress does not altogether oppose the idea of women as combatants is suggested by the legislative histories pertaining to the Equal Rights Amendment and, more recently, to the admission of women to military academies.

The Equal Rights Amendment

In the former case, Senator Sam Ervin attempted to amend the Equal Rights Amendment in 1972:

This article shall not impair the validity, however, of any laws of the United States or any State which exempt women from service in combat units of the Armed Forces.[7]

Arguing passionately to "prevent sending the daughters of America into combat, to be slaughtered or maimed by the bayonets, the bombs, the bullets, the grenades, the mines, the napalm, the poison gas, and the shells of the enemy,"[8] Senator Ervin provided the Senate with the opportunities both to reaffirm the exclusion of women from combat ships and combat aircraft and also to establish explicitly the exclusion of women from ground combat units. Ervin's amendment, however, was defeated by the wide margin of 71 to 18. His companion amendment to exempt women from the military draft was also defeated by 73 to 18.[9]

Admission of Women to the Military Academies

But in 1975 came the strongest signal yet that Congress endorses an expanded role for women in the military. Indeed, it suggests that Congress may no longer consider combat to be a male monopoly.

7. *Congressional Record,* vol. 118, pt. 7 (1972), p. 9337.
8. Ibid.
9. Ibid., pp. 9336, 9351. The interpretation of these results has been the subject of some controversy. One school of thought suggests that the amendments were offered by opponents of the ERA simply to make the equal rights issue less popular. By diluting the egalitarian principle, it is held, the ERA would become less attractive to state legislators, who would question why women should be given equal protection in all other respects, while remaining exempt from combat service. ERA proponents, so the argument goes, were thus all the more adamant to maintain the bill in its "pure" form. (See George H. Quester, "Women in Combat," *International Security,* vol. 1 [Spring 1977], pp. 82–83).

A second school of thought argues that the courts would be likely to take the congressional mandate at face value. Those who opposed Senator Ervin, according to this view, did so to demonstrate that they gave the principle of sexual equality a higher priority than they did the question of women in combat. If they were merely interested in obtaining state ratification for an amendment that provided equality for women in all walks of life save the military, they would have joined Senator Ervin, and avoided one of the most controversial of the ERA issues. The fact that they opposed Ervin, this school argues, shows that they would rather let the issue of women in combat serve as a drag on the amendment at the state level than have an "all-but-combat" ERA.

The Pentagon's principal line of defense in opposing legislation to remove restrictions against women's entrance into the nation's military academies was the inseparability of the academy issue and the combat question. According to General Weyand, the Army's vice chief of staff:

> The issue of whether women should become cadets at West Point is tied directly to the basic question of whether Americans are prepared to commit their daughters to combat. . . .
> The Military Academy has, indeed, the distinctive and necessary mission of educating and training [and] preparing . . . officers for combat roles. . . .
> As long as it is the desire of our people, expressed through the Congress, that women not be employed in combat roles or positions, it seems to me that it would be a waste of a scarce and costly resource to divert any of the Academy's capability to a secondary and lesser mission.[10]

On the floor of the House, the views of those who agreed with the Pentagon were boiled down to the following comment by Representative Lawrence McDonald of Georgia:

> It is therefore obvious that the combat issue is not a false one; it is indeed the central question. If we do not wish our women to serve in combat roles, we should not have them attend our academies.[11]

The amendment to permit women to enter the military academies passed resoundingly, however—303 to 96.[12] On the Senate side, a similar amendment introduced by Senator William Hathaway ran into little difficulty; with the support of Senators John Stennis, Strom Thurmond, and Sam Nunn—all strong Pentagon supporters—the amendment was passed by voice vote.[13]

The broad support in both the Senate and the House stemmed from a coalition of those, on the one hand, who felt that the academy and combat questions were separate issues and of those, on the other hand, who did not object to the idea of women combatants. However, it is impossible to specify how many were in each category.

Several congressmen have sought to meet the combat issue frontally. Three other amendments were introduced in the Ninety-fourth Congress "to prohibit the exclusion, solely on the basis of sex, of women members

10. "Testimony of General Fred C. Weyand," *H.R. 9832 to Eliminate Discrimination Based on Sex with respect to the Appointment and Admission of Persons to the Service Academies,* Hearing before Subcommittee No. 2 of the House Armed Services Committee, 93:1 (GPO, 1975), p. 166.

11. *Congressional Record,* daily ed., May 20, 1975, pp. H4438-39.

12. Ibid., p. 4441.

13. *Congressional Record,* daily ed., June 6, 1975, pp. S9892–95.

of the armed forces from duty involving combat." All were referred to the House Armed Services Committee, where they died.[14]

All of this suggests that women's greater participation in the armed forces has strong congressional support. However, it leaves the combat issue still in limbo.

Judicial Opinion

Judicial trends must also be taken into account. The women's movement has challenged long-held distinctions based on sex and has caused the courts to focus more sharply on the rationales for these distinctions. As a consequence the basis for treating women differently from men in the military has come under closer judicial scrutiny: does traditional "equal protection" analysis suffice to dispose of the new kinds of cases presented to courts by the military personnel policies?

Is Sex a "Suspect Classification"?

During the early 1970s a number of women challenged the military's policy of mandatory discharge for pregnant females. In two cases, federal district courts found military necessity a rational basis for the regulations and ruled that the practice did not deprive women of equal protection of the laws.[15]

However, another federal district court found that that policy did deprive women of due process of law.[16] Although acknowledging the necessity of taking some administrative action to preclude pregnant women from impeding the military mission, the court suggested the possibility of less drastic alternatives, such as reassignments within the service. Before the Supreme Court could resolve the conflict in lower court rulings, abandonment of the mandatory discharge policy rendered the issue moot.

14. H.R. 58 was introduced by Charles H. Wilson, representative from California, on January 14, 1975; H.R. 2190 by California's Congressman Don Edwards on January 28, 1975; and H.R. 12649 by Lawrence Coughlin, representative from Pennsylvania, on March 18, 1976. See U.S. House of Representatives, *Legislative Calendar,* House Armed Services Committee Final Calendar 1975–1976 (GPO, 1976), pp. 13, 26, 73.

15. *Struck* v. *Secretary of Defense,* 460 F 2d 1372 (9th Cir. 1971); *Gutierrez* v. *Laird,* 346 F. Supp. 289 (D.D.C. 1972).

16. *Robinson* v. *Rand,* 340 F. Supp. 37 (D. Colo. 1972).

Soon the Supreme Court confronted another legal challenge to sex discrimination. In *Frontiero* v. *Richardson,* a female Air Force officer challenged a statutory scheme that denied certain dependents' benefits to married women officers.[17] The traditional equal protection argument would have sustained the policy upon showing that the policy was rationally related to a permissible governmental objective (that is, the support of dependent wives in a predominantly male military organization). Eight justices vindicated the position of the female officer, although they were split on the rationale. Four declared sex to be a "suspect classification," thus triggering a requirement that the governmental policy be supported by a "compelling governmental purpose" rather than a mere rational relation to a permissible objective. Four other members of the Court, without relying upon that argument, held that the government had failed to make a sufficiently strong showing of any rational basis for the distinction between dependency benefits accorded male officers and their female counterparts. One justice dissented.[18]

In a subsequent case, it became clear that a majority of the Supreme Court would not regard sex as a suspect classification, at least when dealing with the armed forces. The male plaintiff in *Schlesinger* v. *Ballard,* a naval officer with nine years of service, challenged a statute that mandated his separation for twice failing of promotion; he grounded his equal protection challenge on the fact that the statutory scheme for similarly situated women precluded their involuntary discharge until completion of thirteen years of service.[19]

In a five-to-four decision, a majority of the Supreme Court rejected the view previously held by four justices in the *Frontiero* decision that sex is suspect as a basis for classification, thus sparing the Navy the burden of finding a "compelling governmental justification" for discrimination. Examining the purpose behind the statutory distinction, the Court found that restrictions upon sea duty for women provided them with fewer promotional opportunities, and that the statutory preclusion of mandatory discharge if they were not promoted within thirteen years was designed to

17. *Frontiero* v. *Richardson,* 411 U.S. 677 (1973).

18. Justice William J. Brennan, Jr., speaking for four justices, asserted that classifications based on sex were inherently suspect and thus required close scrutiny; Justice William H. Rehnquist dissented; Justice Potter Stewart stated that he would reverse in this particular instance but did not support Justice Brennan's view; and the other three justices refused to decide whether sex is a suspect classification. See *Frontiero* v. *Richardson,* 411 U.S. 677 (1973).

19. *Schlesinger* v. *Ballard,* 419 U.S. 498 (1975).

compensate for this lack of promotional opportunity. Accordingly, the majority found a rational basis for permitting mandatory separation of males but not of females prior to thirteen years of service. In other words, the Court was prepared to uphold a policy that discriminated against a few men on a relatively peripheral matter (mandatory discharge for failure of promotion) in order to preserve a substantial discrimination against women (preclusion of service aboard ships).

On the other hand, the question continues to be pressed in the lower courts. In *United States* v. *Reiser,* the male defendant, having been indicted for failure to submit to induction into the armed forces, claimed that the Selective Service laws "create a sex-based classification" that burdens only the male, thus depriving him of his rights to equal protection of the laws under the due process clause of the fifth amendment."[20] The Montana district court dismissed the indictment, concluding "that sex is a suspect classification and that the higher standard of strict scrutiny must be applied to the statute."[21] In January 1976, however, the Ninth Circuit Court of Appeals reversed the decision, remanding the case to the district court.[22]

Also, in November 1976, four Navy women filed a class action suit in the U.S. District Court, District of Columbia, asking that the federal statute that prohibits them from serving aboard naval vessels be ruled unconstitutional.[23]

It is therefore still unclear in which direction the judiciary is likely to move in cases of sex discrimination. The decisions to date have been ambivalent especially in regard to the military.

What Would Be the Effect of ERA?

Sexual distinctions within the military will probably be subjected to much closer judicial scrutiny if the Equal Rights Amendment is ratified. According to one view:

The Equal Rights Amendment will result in substantial changes in our military institutions. The number of women serving, and the positions they occupy, will be far greater than at present. Women will be subject to the draft, and the requirements for enlistment will be the same for both sexes. In-service and

20. 394 F. Supp. 1060 (D. Mont. 1975).
21. Ibid.
22. 532 F 2d 673 (9th Cir. 1976).
23. *Owens* v. *Rumsfeld,* Civil No. 76-2086, U.S. District Court, District of Columbia, November 10, 1976.

veterans' benefits will be identical. Women will serve in all kinds of units, and they will be eligible for combat duty.[24]

Other commentators, however, have suggested that the ERA would merely designate sex as a "suspect classification," which would allow the courts to sustain discriminatory practices in the military if the distinctions were supported by "a compelling government interest." As one observer notes:

> Sex discrimination as such could still be tolerated in some situations where it comes into direct conflict with another fundamental constitutional right, such as the "penumbra" right to privacy or the right of the nation to protect and defend itself under the constitutional war powers. Therefore, if the constitutional immunities granted to individuals of both sexes under the Equal Rights Amendment are outweighed by some other constitutional right or power, the latter will have to take precedence.[25]

Still another commentator, drawing on the sex discrimination litigation involving the Equal Employment Opportunity Commission, has suggested that the ERA would not preclude distinctions based on sex if they were based upon a bona fide occupational qualification.[26]

For the present at least, while the courts may no longer view laws pertaining to the military to be valid per se, extensive judicial involvement with the thorny issue of the sex composition of the armed forces appears unlikely. Thus, in the absence of strong pressure by the legislature or the judiciary, prospects for expanding women's participation in the armed forces may depend largely on attitudes within the military itself.

Military Attitudes

How the defense establishment, and particularly its military leadership, perceives the role of women is certain to weigh heavily in shaping future policies. Reaction by military leaders to the general concept of expanding women's participation in the armed services has so far ranged between ambivalence and acclamation; few have publicly opposed the idea.

24. Barbara A. Brown and others, "The Equal Rights Amendment: A Constitutional Basis for Equal Rights for Women," *The Yale Law Journal*, vol. 80 (April 1971), p. 978.

25. David B. Ratterman, "Fourteenth Amendment Practice in Sex Discrimination Cases," *Journal of Family Law*, Louisville School of Law, vol. 14 (1975–1976), p. 460.

26. See Harry G. Beans, "Sex Discrimination in the Military," *Military Law Review*, vol. 67 (Winter 1975), p. 72.

Despite recent changes, women still constitute a relatively small proportion of total military strength and for the most part remain assigned—by design or by choice—to "feminine" jobs. However, further expansion will require that women transgress on traditionally male occupations and at some point on combat and seagoing assignments, a prospect that would be less than welcomed by traditionalists in the military establishment.

Where the services would draw the battle line and how hard they would fight to protect their male prerogatives are difficult to predict. Some feel that the line may already have been crossed. In September 1976, Colonel Loma Allen, a former chief of the Army's equal opportunity program, stated:

In the past six months or so, I have noticed . . . a regression by Army leadership in its consideration of continuing to open opportunities for women and indeed in holding open those that it had previously considered. . . . The Army was really on a track and was moving down that track in the forefront of American society. [But] my feeling is that the Army has flat put the brakes on and the wheels are spinning backward.[27]

At the extreme, there is little doubt that military leaders are opposed to female encroachment into the combat clique—the essence of the military establishment. That much is apparent in the congressional testimony of military leaders who opposed the enrollment of women in the nation's military academies. Indeed, the parade of Pentagon officials almost unanimously deplored the idea of women as combatants or of females at sea. A former superintendent of the United States Air Force Academy reflected a traditionally paternalistic view:

For this Nation to open combat roles to our women, short of a dire emergency, in my view, offends the dignity of womanhood and ignores the harsh realities of war. Military history, the lessons of which again we ignore at our peril, my own personal experiences in combat, in prisoner of war camps, and in command of units convince me that fighting is a man's job and should remain so. Those who press to inject women in combat roles grossly underestimate the physical, the mental and the emotional stresses of combat in all its implications, including capture by the enemy. In my view Sherman was right: "War is hell and you cannot refine it." To seek to do so to accommodate the pressures of social activism is to invite disaster in battle. Our potential enemies would rejoice to see us make the tragic error of exposing American women to capture in combat. I firmly believe that this situation would inevitably weaken our national resolve in war.[28]

27. Colonel Loma O. Allen, quoted in *Army Times,* September 20, 1976.
28. "Testimony of Lieutenant General A. P. Clark," *H.R. 9832 to Eliminate Discrimination . . . ,* Hearing, pp. 135–36.

The possible loss in military effectiveness was the theme of the testimony given by Secretary Callaway:

At issue is the quality of combat leadership. The severe standards set for the West Point cadet are predicated upon his future role as a combat leader. The Academy's primary mission of preparing battle leaders for our Nation's military forces is accomplished through . . . rigorous, unremitting training. Any reduction of this emphasis in order to accommodate women would in effect lead to a lowering of standards for men. . . . Inevitably, the product of West Point would be altered.[29]

A minority view was presented by Vice Admiral William P. Mack, then superintendent of the U.S. Naval Academy:

In my estimation, women could serve in any role in the U.S. Navy at any time if this law [restricting women from serving aboard naval vessels and combat aircraft] were changed. They could come to the Naval Academy; they could pass the course in large numbers, and do all that's required of them physically, mentally, professionally, and in any other way, and there would be little requirements for change in our course curriculum, physical facilities, or anything of that sort. If the law were changed, in my mind, women could do anything that men could do, and, in some cases, perhaps even better.[30]

Pentagon civilian officials have generally echoed the attitudes of military leaders on this issue and, based on an early reading, Secretary of Defense Harold Brown does not appear to be an exception. Barely six days into his term, Brown provided his views to a congressional committee:

I believe there are sufficient physical differences between men and women, on the average, that make it wise, as regulations provide, that women not be put into combat roles.[31]

29. "Testimony of Howard H. Callaway, Secretary of the Army," ibid., pp. 161–62.

30. "Testimony of Vice Admiral P. Mack, Superintendent, U.S. Naval Academy," ibid., p. 96. Admiral Mack, however, did not support striking down the restrictions imposed in Title 10:

. . . despite my belief that some women could perform many combat roles as well as men, I am personally and philosophically opposed to the repeal of the statute which precludes their use in combat roles in the Navy, at sea and in the air. So, too, am I opposed to the admission of women to the Naval Academy without repeal of the restrictions on their assignability to sea and air roles. Therefore, I must conclude that the all-male admissions policy which presently obtains at the Naval Academy is correct, now and for the foreseeable future (ibid., p. 128).

31. *Fiscal Year 1978 Authorization for Military Procurement, Research and Development, and Active Duty, Selected Reserve and Civilian Personnel Strengths,* Hearings before the Senate Committee on Armed Services, 95:1 (GPO, 1977), pt. 1, p. 533.

Retired senior military officials are often a better barometer of the military hierarchy's real attitudes toward policy questions. Unfettered from congressional decorum and no longer subject to rigid rules of bureaucratic propriety, these officials are more likely to speak candidly.

For example, General William C. Westmoreland, former Army chief of staff, acknowledging that he never would have made such a statement while on active duty, said bluntly:

> Maybe you could find one woman in 10,000 who could lead in combat, but she would be a freak and we're not running the military academy for freaks. . . . The pendulum has gone too far. . . . They're asking women to do impossible things. I don't believe women can carry a pack, live in a foxhole, or go a week without taking a bath.[32]

In an alternate view, former Chief of Naval Operations Admiral Elmo R. Zumwalt spoke out in support of an expanded role for women. They should, he said, "have the opportunity to . . . go into combat . . . and as far as women soldiers are concerned, when I was in Southeast Asia during the Vietnam war I found that among the most vicious fighters were the Viet Cong women."[33] It is widely known, however, that Admiral Zumwalt was and continues to be at odds with Navy traditionalists.

Thus, although the military leadership will attempt to protect its masculine essence, it seems likely that a further modest increase in the number of women in the military would not be met with undue alarm. Even General Westmoreland, in a departure from his otherwise acerbic assessment of women's potential, hedgingly allowed: "There are plenty of jobs they can do without going to excesses."[34]

Some might speculate that attitudes toward women are likely to change in the future as the products of a more progressive generation replace the existing old guard. Even if the current crop of young military men were more favorably disposed toward egalitarian principles, however, the likelihood that leadership attitudes will change in future generations is probably small. There is no denying that the military promotion system serves to perpetuate traditional doctrine through what one observer describes as "a continuous selection of people with the 'right' attitudes within the profession, since the chances for promotion are not equal but tend to favor candidates who conform to their superior's expectations."[35]

32. *Washington Post,* May 30, 1976.
33. *Washington Post,* September 21, 1976.
34. *Washington Post,* May 30, 1976.
35. Bengt Abrahamsson, *Military Professionalization and Political Power* (Sage Publications, 1972), p. 74.

How the rank and file perceive these issues can also be expected to influence the future role of women in the military. Over the last several years, numerous surveys have been made to assess the attitudes of military personnel. Because of variations in purpose and design and because the polls were taken during a period of rapidly changing attitudes, it is difficult to interrelate the results. Nevertheless, some general conclusions emerge:

1. Not surprisingly, military men are more conservative than military women. While more women than men tend to describe themselves as contemporary (egalitarian), a large proportion of both men and women consider the majority of military women to be contemporary and the majority of military men to be traditional. Moreover, the way men viewed themselves was strikingly different from the way they were viewed by other men and women.[36]

2. The majority of military personnel appear to support greater participation by women. Although variations exist in the attitudes between the sexes, and between officers and enlisted personnel, on balance, most noncombat jobs—including those traditionally held by men—are judged to be also appropriate for women. As would be expected, female officers and, to a lesser extent, enlisted women perceive a wider range of jobs falling within their capabilities. And although male military personnel are somewhat more skeptical, a majority appears to favor using more women in the service and the liberalization of military policies.[37]

3. A series of surveys indicate that military personnel are not strongly antagonistic to the assignment of women to combat units or aboard naval vessels. The majority of both men and women seem to favor the concept in principle, but there is less support among men. Moreover, many of the

36. See Joel M. Savell and Barry Collins, *Soldiers' Attribution of Contemporary vs. Traditional Sex-Role Attitudes to Themselves and to Others,* Research Memorandum 75-7 (U.S. Army Research Institute for the Behavioral and Social Sciences, July 1975); Patricia J. Thomas and Kathleen P. Durning, "The Military Woman and the Navy Wife," Paper presented to the Eighty-fourth Annual Convention of the American Psychological Association, Washington, D.C. (San Diego, Calif.: Navy Personnel Research and Development Center [NPRDC], September 1976; processed). "Utilization of Women in Industrial Career Fields," information sheet provided by the U.S. Air Force (n.d.; processed).

37. See: Joel M. Savell, John C. Woelfel, and Barry Collins, *Attitudes Concerning Job Appropriateness for Women in the Army,* Research Memorandum 75-3 (U.S. Army Research Institute for the Behavioral and Social Sciences, June 1975); Thomas and Durning, "The Military Woman and the Navy Wife"; "Utilization of Women in Industrial Career Fields"; and Air Force Management Improvement Group, survey extract (Department of the Air Force, September 1976; processed).

women who endorse a combat role for women do not appear to want such a role for themselves.[38]

It should also be remembered that the infusion of women into the armed services and particularly into nontraditional occupations is a relatively recent phenomenon. The attitudes of military personnel toward women may change as more women enter the armed forces. As experience with racial integration attests, the attitudes of whites toward accepting blacks were found to be related to previous contact. In fact, one study indicated that "whites' attitudes toward accepting Negroes became increasingly positive as a direct function of the extent of desegregation attempted."[39] More recently, researchers began to explore the hypothesis that "as men become more accustomed to women in the workplace, they will become more accepting of them as well."[40]

ALL IN ALL, the foregoing analysis underscores the ambivalence of national attitudes toward the role of women in the armed forces. With respect to this issue, the so-called will of the American people proves to be elusive, judicial opinion is unclear, attitudes within Congress are not sharply drawn, and the reactions of the military establishment, which is still suffering "growing pains" on the issue of sex integration, have escaped reliable assessment.

In the face of evidence, as sparse as it is, it appears unlikely that the public, the judiciary, the legislature, or the military would strongly oppose further expansion in the number and role of women in the armed forces—up to a point. Whether or not these institutions are—or should be—prepared to break with long tradition and condone women as combatants or aboard naval vessels is a tougher issue, which is discussed in chapter 7.

38. See, for example, Kathleen Durning and Sandra Mumford, *Differential Perceptions of Organizational Climate Held by Navy Enlisted Women and Men* NPRDC TR 76 TQ-43 (NPRDC, 1976; processed); David R. Segal and others "The Concept of Citizenship and Attitudes toward Women in Combat" (Arlington, Va.: Army Research Institute for Behavioral and Social Sciences, 1975; processed); Patricia J. Thomas, "Utilization of Enlisted Women in the Military" (NPRDC, 1976; processed); Thomas and Durning, "The Military Woman and the Navy Wife"; and *USAF Survey of Women Line Officers,* Management Analysis Report 73-1 (Department of the Air Force [AF/ACM], 1973).

39. Joseph M. Notterman, *Behavior: A Systematic Approach* (Random House, 1970), pp. 328–29.

40. David R. Segal and John C. Woelfel, "Interacting with Women: Interpersonal Contact and Acceptance of Women in the U.S. Army," Research Memorandum 76-5 (U.S. Army Research Institute for the Behavioral and Social Sciences, April 1976; processed), p. 1.

CHAPTER SIX

THE ECONOMICS OF SEX INTEGRATION

While social forces must be considered in the development of national policies with respect to women in the military, so too must a dollars-and-cents, cost-effectiveness test. What mix of military men and women can meet U.S. national security needs at the lowest cost? If an increase in the proportion of women in the military could lead to lower costs without sacrificing effectiveness, the United States is paying more than is necessary to field its present military forces. The financial implications associated with a change in the mix of men and women in the armed forces are discussed below. (The other side of the coin—the implications for the effectiveness of U.S. military forces—is examined in chapter 7.)

What are the comparative costs of recruiting and maintaining military men and women in the armed forces and why do they differ? First, there are the one-time costs associated with modifying or building facilities to meet privacy standards and redesigning clothing and equipment. Second are the costs of dependents; military women are less likely to be married than their male contemporaries and, on average, have fewer dependents. Third are possible differences in retention patterns; more frequent turnover leads to larger acquisition, training, and separation costs. And, fourth, there are the effects of increasing the total supply of qualified volunteers on the average price of military manpower.

One-time Adjustment Costs

The cost of constructing or modifying housing and lavatory facilities to ensure privacy has been a dominant—and often exclusive—consideration in much of the public debate about increasing the number of women in the military. Certainly, unless the services are willing to make some concessions, the costs will be higher than necessary. For example, current Air Force policy, which prevents the joint use of hallways in sexually integrated barracks, should be reassessed. Overall, though, these costs are relatively insignificant. In many cases, more flexible use of existing facilities would answer the purpose. Why military barracks facilities cannot be modified to a coeducational configuration in much the same fashion as college dormitories has not been adequately explained.

In some instances, such as berthing women on naval vessels, the costs would be greater. According to the Department of the Navy, the total cost of modifying all active naval vessels to accommodate women crewmembers would range from $96 million, if women were to constitute 4 percent of the crews, to about $132 million, if the proportion were 20 percent. Aircraft carriers would require the least modification; the Navy estimates that it could outfit all carriers to accommodate crews of which one-fifth were women for about $400,000.[1]

Potentially more important, but not as widely recognized, are the one-time costs associated with redesigning special clothing and equipment. In particular, the assignment of women to traditionally male occupations could require extensive changes. For example, Army equipment is generally designed for men with anthropometric dimensions ranging from the 5th through the 95th percentiles of all men; thus men whose measurements fall in the top and bottom 5 percent of the male population are not accommodated. In a number of critical dimensions—weight, stature, sitting height, eye height, popliteal height (floor to thigh while seated), functional reach and foot length—the average woman measures significantly less than the average man. For example, among women aged eighteen to twenty-four years, about 45 percent weigh less than a man at the 5th percentile (124 pounds) in the same age group, about 60 percent are shorter (64.3 inches), about 30 percent have a shorter sitting height (31.9 inches), and about one-half have a shorter popliteal height (16 inches).[2] According to one researcher, although differences may appear insignificant, "seemingly minor variations of a few centimeters in the

1. *Hearings on H.R. 9832, to Eliminate Discrimination Based on Sex with Respect to the Appointment and Admission of Persons to the Service Academies,* House Armed Services Committee, 93:2 (GPO, 1974), pp. 118–19.

2. U.S. Department of Health, Education, and Welfare, Public Health Service, *Weight, Height, and Selected Body Dimensions of Adults, United States 1960–62,* Data from the National Health Survey, Series 11, No. 8 (HEW, June 1965), pp. 26, 27, 29, 31. (In May 1977 these were the latest data available on anthropometric dimensions of the general population.)

essential dimensions . . . may be critical determinants in the efficient and safe usage of vehicles and vehicular subsystems, controls, instrument panels, displays, etc., and in the adequate accommodation of some clothing and protective gear."[3]

It is difficult to make even an intelligent guess about the extent to which military equipment would have to be redesigned and the expenditures that might eventually be involved. But it requires closer examination, particularly as women move into activities for which materiel designs are currently geared to their larger and stronger male counterparts. Also needing further investigation are the consequences of designing future aircraft, tanks, and other weapons to accommodate smaller, lighter women. Often cost and performance penalties are associated with designing for larger heavier crewmembers.

Cost of Dependents

Military personnel with families are paid more and enjoy more benefits than those who are single, even when they do the same job. Moreover, the cost to the government of providing some services bears a relationship to family size. Women now have fewer dependents on average (see table 6-1) than men and therefore use these services less. The largest differences occur in housing allowances, medical benefits, and the cost of moving people and their households.[4]

Housing Costs

When facilities are available, military personnel live in housing provided by the government. Single individuals are generally billeted in barracks or officers' quarters not unlike college dormitories. Married personnel, on the other hand, are provided with apartments, townhouses, or detached homes similar to many found in the private sector. The quality of accommodations varies considerably, however, even among those personnel having the same grade and dependency status. Although the differential is difficult to measure precisely, the cost to the government of

3. Monica M. Glumm, *The Female in Military Equipment Design,* Technical Memorandum 13-76 (U.S. Army Engineering Laboratory, April 1976), p. 2.
4. For a further discussion of the cost of supporting military dependents, see Martin Binkin, *The Military Pay Muddle* (Brookings Institution, 1975).

Table 6-1. Number of Dependents of Military Personnel, by Sex, December 1975

Dependency characteristic and class	Men	Women	Total
Total military personnel	**1,966,475**	**103,802**	**2,070,277**
Officers	268,834	13,795	282,629
Enlisted	1,697,641	90,007	1,787,648
Number of military personnel with dependents	1,127,037	22,546	1,149,583
Officers	221,953	3,082	225,035
Enlisted	905,084	19,464	924,548
Number of dependents of military personnel	2,817,015	28,510	2,845,525
Officers	618,699	3,409	622,108
Enlisted	2,198,316	25,101	2,223,417
Military personnel with dependents as a percent of total military personnel	57.3	21.7	55.5
Officers	82.6	22.3	79.6
Enlisted	53.3	21.6	51.7
Average number of dependents per military person with dependents	2.50	1.26	2.48
Officers	2.79	1.10	2.76
Enlisted	2.43	1.29	2.40
Average number of dependents per military person	1.43	0.27	1.37
Officers	2.30	0.25	2.20
Enlisted	1.29	0.28	1.24

Source: Derived from data provided by the Office of the Assistant Secretary of Defense for Manpower and Reserve Affairs, August 1976.

providing family housing far exceeds the cost of providing bachelor quarters.

More easily measured are the cash allowances paid to those with and without dependents when government housing is not available.[5] Cash "quarters allowances," based on rank and dependency status, are periodically adjusted. In May 1977, they ranged from $73.80 a month for an unmarried recruit to $371.40 a month for a general or flag officer with dependents. The amount by which the cash allowances paid to those with dependents exceeds the allowances paid to those without dependents varies by rank; the differential ranges from 20 to 75 percent. Army captains with dependents, for example, received $45.90 a month more than captains without dependents; for Army corporals, on the other hand, the amount was $48.60.

5. Information on quarters allowances is from data provided by the Office of the Assistant Secretary of Defense for Manpower and Reserve Affairs, May 1977.

The average difference in the quarters allowance of those with and without dependents is $52 a month (based on cash rates). Since about 36 percent fewer women have dependents, they are about $225 a year less costly to the military than men. The dollar difference is more striking when government accommodations are available, since it generally costs the government more to provide individual and family quarters than cash allowances.

Medical Costs

A large part of the cost of the military health services system is related to the medical care provided to dependents of active-duty and retired military personnel. In fiscal 1975, for example, 60 percent of the total beneficiary population were dependents, and, of the total care provided in the continental United States, dependents accounted for 50 and 54 percent of the inpatient and outpatient workloads, respectively.[6] The medical benefits available to dependents are described in chapter 4. On average, the cost to the government of providing health service amounts to roughly $300 per dependent per year.[7] Thus the typical military male, who has 1.16 more dependents than the typical female, costs about $350 a year more for medical support.

Travel Costs

Travel costs incurred when a single person is reassigned are also far less than the cost of moving a family. The variation is due mainly to differences in the weight of household goods, which are shipped at government expense. In fiscal 1977, for example, the average cost to move an Air Force officer without dependents from one duty assignment to another within the United States was estimated at $314 ($146 mileage and per diem and $168 dislocation allowance).[8] For officers with dependents, the

6. Department of Defense, Department of Health, Education, and Welfare, Office of Management and Budget, *Report of the Military Health Care Study* (GPO, December 1975), pp. 25–27.

7. Based on an estimate provided by the Department of Defense, Office of the Assistant Secretary of Defense for Health and Environment, October 1974, updated by the authors to account for the effects of inflation.

8. Department of Defense, "Fiscal Year 1977 Permanent Change of Station Travel" (DOD, January 1976; processed). Dislocation allowances, which are equivalent to one month's quarters allowance, are intended to defray the incidental expenses (for example, motel charges while house hunting) associated with dislocating.

average cost was over $3,000 more—$233 mileage and per diem for dependents and about $2,780 to ship household goods. For the entire Department of Defense, because of differences in the proportions of personnel with dependents, the average cost of moving a woman is roughly $407 a year less than the average cost of moving a man.[9]

Total Possible Savings

As summarized in table 6-2, the average annual per capita cost associated with these three factors—housing, medical care, and transportation—is estimated to be about $982 less for military women than for men.[10] Thus, based on differences in dependency status alone, the cost to the Department of Defense of the average military woman is now about 8 percent less than the average military man whose cost is about $11,700 a year. Whether this difference would persist if a greater number of women were admitted to the military services is uncertain. As shown in chapter 2, of those women who have volunteered over the past several years, a surprisingly large proportion (about 10 percent) have been married. If this situation continued and if a large share of married women were to reenlist, the present dependency-related cost differences would disappear.

Attrition, Absenteeism, and Retirement

Personnel turnover also affects costs: the shorter the period of time that the average person remains in the military, the greater the cost to maintain armed forces of a certain size. New entrants must be recruited,

9. Based on the following information calculated from the Department of Defense, "Fiscal Year 1977 Permanent Change of Station Travel":

Type of reassignment	Probability of reassignment in 1977	Average additional cost of moving families (dollars)
Operational (stateside)	0.083	1,705
Rotational (overseas)	0.241	2,297
Training	0.095	1,655
Separation	0.239	1,219

Hence $(0.083 \times 1,705) + (0.241 \times 2,297) + (0.095 \times 1,655) + (0.239 \times 1,219)$
      $= 1,144 \times 0.356$ (35.6 percent fewer women have dependents) $= 407$.
Figures are calculated for total military personnel.

10. This estimate is rough. The list of dependent-related costs is not exhaustive; not included are costs associated with dependent education, commissaries, and the

Table 6-2. Estimated Average Annual per Capita Savings in Dependent-Related Costs from Recruitment of Women instead of Men

Dollars

Dependent-cost category	Estimated savings
Housing allowance	225
Medical care	350
Transportation	407
Total savings	982

Source: Authors' estimates.

processed, trained, moved to operational units, and then trained on the job. Moreover, those leaving the service must be processed and moved from their last duty station. All of these functions absorb defense dollars, and, to a certain point, reductions in the rate of turnover would lead to lower total costs.

Attrition

A combination of factors influences the average length of time that people remain in the service. The most important are the duration of the first enlistment period, attrition rates during that period, and retention patterns beyond the first enlistment.

Traditionally, one of the strongest arguments against expanding the number of women in the military has been their tendency to leave the service before completing their first enlistment. In large measure, greater attrition among women was a consequence of service policies regarding marriage and pregnancy. Until recently, women could request discharges if they married, and they were involuntarily separated if they became pregnant. As late as 1972, about one-third of all enlisted women who separated from the services left for reasons of marriage or pregnancy.

The pronounced effects of these policies are shown in table 6-3, which compares the average duration of military service for men and women based on experience during the sixties. To sustain a force of constant size, the Air Force and the Navy would have had to train two women for every man to be replaced. However, since the military services have changed

like. Also not reflected is the fact that some military personnel are married to each other. An accurate count has not been taken, but based on 1973 Air Force survey data, about 30 percent of married Air Force enlisted women are married to military men. U.S. Air Force, "United States Air Force Survey of Enlisted Women" (March 1973; processed).

Table 6-3. Average Years Served by Enlisted Personnel, by Sex, Fiscal Years 1960–70
Years

Military service	Men	Women
Army	3.4	2.2
Navy	4.5	2.2
Air Force	5.1	2.6
Marine Corps	2.4	1.7

Source: Central All-Volunteer Task Force, "Utilization of Military Women" (Office of the Assistant Secretary of Defense for Manpower and Reserve Affairs, December 1972; processed).

their policies to permit married and pregnant women to remain and since more liberal discharge policies and a high incidence of disciplinary problems have fostered higher rates of attrition among men, the differences have narrowed dramatically. To illustrate, table 6-4 compares the rates at which men and women have been leaving the services *before* completing their first enlistment period. Highlighting the turnabout has been the proportion not even completing the first year. Men entering the service in fiscal 1975, for example, left during their first year at a rate 55 percent greater than those who had entered four years earlier; the rate at which women departed between 1971 and 1975 declined by about one-third.[11]

Moreover, since the average duration of initial enlistment over the past several years has been approximately the same for both men and women (as shown in table 2-3), the expected years of service for women, given the present course, could well exceed that of men. In fact, as early as 1974, the average woman entering the Air Force was expected to serve 4.64 years compared with 4.46 years for the average man.[12]

11. Attrition rates differ according to occupation. They tend to be higher for both sexes in their respective nontraditional fields. For example, of all the women who entered the electronic equipment repair specialty in fiscal 1973, only 24 percent remained at the end of fiscal 1976, whereas the comparable figure for males was 49 percent. In maintenance, the corresponding proportions were 10 percent for women and 47 percent for men. The opposite relationship holds in traditionally "feminine" occupations. In the administrative area, for instance, 70 percent of the women who entered in fiscal 1973 were still employed at the end of 1976, compared with 40 percent of the men. The fact that proportionately more women in nontraditional skills are either leaving the service or migrating to other occupations may be related to the practice of assigning many women to nontraditional skills who were unqualified. This situation is discussed further in chapter 7. (Office of the Assistant Secretary of Defense for Manpower and Reserve Affairs, "Use of Women in the Military," background study [OASD, Manpower and Reserve Affairs, May 1977; processed], p. 12.)

12. United States Air Force, Directorate of Personnel Plans, "Women in the Air Force: Are They Cost Effective?" (April 1975; processed).

Table 6-4. Percentage of Total Military Personnel Not Completing First Enlistment Period, by Duration of Service and Sex, Fiscal Years 1971–75

Percent

Duration of service, by sex	1971	1972	1973	1974	1975
Less than one year					
Male	11.1	11.9	12.4	17.3	17.1
Female	24.7	20.9	17.4	17.9	15.6
One-to-two years					
Male	7.5	8.6	10.8	10.6	...
Female	18.7	16.5	14.9	10.4	...
Two-to-three years					
Male	3.8	6.1	6.7	...	...
Female	8.0	8.6	7.2	...	...

Source: Data provided by Assistant Secretary of Defense for Manpower and Reserve Affairs, September 1976.

The changes in policy that brought these improvements, however, have given rise to costs of their own. As discussed earlier, women who now become pregnant after entering the services are retained unless they request to be separated.[13] Women who choose to remain in the Army, for example, may be placed on "sick in quarters" status during the prenatal period for not more than four weeks and during the postpartum period they are authorized convalescent leave not to exceed six weeks. According to the Army, however, each pregnancy carried to term in fiscal 1976 resulted in an average of 105 days of lost time.[14]

Data concerning pregnancies are not routinely collected by the military services. According to the Army, about 8 percent of Army women become pregnant each year. The Air Force has reported a similar incidence. Based on a survey covering a recent twelve-month period, the Army estimated that about 200,000 days were lost as a result of pregnancies and the Navy about 25,000.[15] The associated costs are hard to measure. To the extent that a unit is under strength as a result of this lost time, there is apt to be a loss in productivity. In some cases—for example, for persons traveling between assignments or for hospitalized

13. In addition to the financial costs discussed here, changes in these policies have implications for military effectiveness, which are discussed in chapter 7.

14. Data provided by the Department of the Army, September 1976.

15. OASD, Manpower and Reserve Affairs, "Use of Women in the Military," pp. 3–16, 26, and Department of the Army, Office of the Deputy Chief of Personnel, "Women in the Army Study" (Department of the Army, December 1976; processed), chap. 7.

patients—the armed services are provided with extra personnel to offset lost time. If that policy were adopted for pregnancies, one extra person would have to be provided for every 90 women in the Army and for every 275 women in the Navy.

Absenteeism

Concern has also been expressed that military women tend to have a higher rate of absenteeism because of illness. Reliable data are hard to obtain; since there is no limitation on the amount of sick leave that military personnel can take, these statistics are not maintained. Some of the concern may stem from experience in the private sector, however, where women are found to lose slightly more time to illness than men. For example, in 1974, women were absent for illness an average of 5.1 days a year compared to 4.8 days for men.[16] Factors other than sex should be considered, however, since women are more likely to be newly hired or in less skilled and less well-paid positions—groups in which absenteeism for illness runs higher than the norm.

It is equally important, on the other hand, to compare time lost by men and women for reasons other than illness, such as disciplinary incidents, drug abuse, and alcoholism. The services do not routinely break down disciplinary statistics by sex, but a few figures have been documented. For example, while women constituted 4.9 percent of total Air Force personnel in fiscal 1975, they received only 1.3 percent of all courts-martial and 2.7 percent of all administrative reprimands.[17] And, with women constituting 12.5 percent of the ship's company aboard the U.S.S. *Sanctuary* (an experiment discussed in chapter 7), they accounted for but 6.9 percent of the disciplinary cases presented at "captain's mast."[18]

Though the data are sparse, they do support the conventional view that women have a greater tendency than men to respect authority and to cause fewer disciplinary problems. Moreover, since a greater propor-

16. Department of Health, Education, and Welfare, Public Health Service, *Current Estimates from the Health Interview Survey, United States—1974,* Data from the National Health Survey, Series 10, No. 100 (HEW, September 1975), p. 22.

17. Data provided by the Department of the Air Force, September 1976.

18. "Evaluation of Women Aboard the U.S.S. *Sanctuary*" (Memorandum from the Commanding Officer, U.S.S. *Sanctuary* [AH-7] to Chief of Naval Personnel, November 19, 1973), pp. 2-3, 4-3, 4-4. Some skeptics argue that lower disciplinary rates among women are partly a consequence of greater leniency by male supervisors toward women than toward men.

tion of military men than women have not completed high school—a factor that appears to be highly correlated with unauthorized absences (AWOL) and desertion incidents—women can be expected to lose less time on this account. For example, from July through September 1976, the Navy lost about 385,000 days' work because of unauthorized absence or desertion. Less than 1 percent of that time was lost by women, however.[19]

Also, recent increases in the rates of drug and alcoholic abuse in the military services appear to affect a greater proportion of men than women. In 1975, in the Navy alone, an estimated 190,000 days were lost for drug rehabilitation and an additional 196,000 to rehabilitate alcoholics. Of the total time lost for both (about 1,058 man-years), women accounted for only 2 percent, even though they constituted about 4 percent of the Navy work force.[20] In a survey of Navy personnel, a far larger proportion of enlisted men (24.3 percent) reported either lost time or reduced efficiency because of drinking compared with enlisted women (15.6 percent).[21]

When all these factors are taken into account, the absentee rate of Navy men is almost twice that of Navy women:[22]

Reason for lost time	Days lost as a percentage of total days available	
	Women	*Men*
Alcohol abuse	0.09	0.12
Drug use	0.02	0.12
Unauthorized absence (AWOL)	0.05	0.24
Desertion	0.07	0.62
Abortion	0.03	. . .
Pregnancy	0.37	. . .
Total	0.63	1.10

However, the same situation prevails as in the case of the relative cost advantages of recruiting women because they have on average fewer dependents. The present cost advantages that women enjoy because of fewer disciplinary, drug, and alcohol problems can be expected to narrow over

19. Data provided by the Department of the Navy, October 1976.
20. Based on data provided by the Department of the Navy, October 1976.
21. Don Calahan and Ira H. Cisin, "Final Report on a Service-wide Survey of Attitudes and Behavior of Naval Personnel Concerning Alcohol and Problem Drinking" (Washington, D.C.: Bureau of Social Science Research, March 3, 1975), pp. 36–38.
22. Data provided by the Department of the Navy, March 1977.

time. Since these problems may be related as much to educational level, general intelligence, and type of duty as they are to gender, their incidence can be expected to increase as additional women, presumably of declining "quality," enter the armed forces and the nontraditional jobs.

Retirement

Another factor related to retention is the potentially greater costs of the military retirement system because women have a longer life expectancy than men. How great this difference will be can only be approximated. Roughly speaking, the annual retirement accrual cost—the amount that would have to be paid into a fund annually to meet expected future retirement obligations—is about 25 percent larger for a woman than for a man.[23] Here again, whether or not women would continue to enjoy a greater life expectancy than men if they entered jobs that subjected them to the same physical and emotional stresses as men is unclear. Some might argue that, as more women pursued nontraditional military careers, their life expectancy might approach that of their male counterparts.

Total Cost of Sustaining Military Women

In sum, the above analysis dispels the widely held belief that military women give rise to higher defense costs than do men. In fact, it demonstrates that, at the present time, it may be less expensive, on average, to sustain women in the military. The more relevant question, however, is how much more or less it would cost if additional women were substituted for men. As more women enter the services, it is likely that the characteristics that now render them less costly would be diluted, and differences in average costs would narrow. On the other hand, the men who would not be recruited because of an increase in women would presumably be the most costly (that is, of lowest quality). As long as the cost associated with an additional woman (that is, the marginal cost) is less than the cost of the man she displaces, the shift would produce financial savings, even though the *average* cost of sustaining women in the services may be rising.

23. Based on a life expectancy at birth of 75.3 years for women and 67.6 years for men. See Department of Health, Education, and Welfare, National Center for Health Statistics, "Monthly Vital Statistics Report," *Final Mortality Statistics, 1973,* vol. 23, no. 11, Supplement 2 (GPO, 1974).

The Recruitment Factor

A more important financial consideration than the relative cost of sustaining men and women under present conditions is the opportunity cost associated with maintaining present recruitment policies in the face of developing demographic and economic trends. There are growing doubts about whether this nation, despite recent large increases in monetary incentives, will be able to sustain an all-volunteer force of appropriate quality. The danger is that the services might systematically exclude capable and available female candidates, even though the search for less qualified men is likely to be an expensive one.

Whether or not male recruiting shortfalls will develop and, if they do, how large they will be hinges foremost on how many new recruits will be needed each year, the qualitative characteristics they are required to possess, the size of the supply pool from which the Pentagon draws its recruits, and the propensity of those qualified to volunteer. The first three factors are reasonably predictable; the last, a function of many interrelated considerations, is highly uncertain.

The armed forces of the United States consist in 1977 of 2.1 million personnel. While some argue for smaller and others for larger standing forces, a broad consensus appears to support the continuation of an active military establishment of roughly 2 million. According to Pentagon calculations, to maintain an armed force of that size under prevailing policies will require that an average of about 365,000 male civilians volunteer each year for military duty. On the face of it, the task appears manageable; 359,000 men were recruited in fiscal 1974—the first full year of the all-volunteer force—367,000 volunteered in fiscal 1975 and 360,000 in fiscal 1976.[24] Given the present trend and circumstances, the rate at which qualified volunteers enlisted during the first three years under a volunteer system would be adequate to meet average long-term needs. But trends and circumstances are changing.

Demographic Trends

As the postwar baby boom runs its course, the pool from which the armed services have traditionally attracted their male volunteers will begin to diminish. A few years from now, as the effects of dwindling birth

24. Data supplied by the Department of Defense, October 1976.

rates in the 1960s are felt, the number of young men reaching eighteen and entering the recruiting target population will decline. The decline will be sharp, reaching 15 percent by 1985 and over 25 percent by 1992, as the following projection of the eighteen-year-old male cohort shows for calendar years 1976–92 (in thousands):[25]

1976	1978	1980	1982	1984	1986	1988	1990	1992
2,147	2,134	2,127	2,068	1,873	1,782	1,850	1,747	1,610

With a smaller source of supply of males, recruiting will become more difficult; how difficult is suggested by a comparison of the proportion of men, among those who are qualified and available, who would have to volunteer for military service to maintain the required rate of accessions.[26] This comparison, shown in table 6-5, indicates that to sustain annual accessions of about 365,000 men, nearly one out of every eleven qualified and available seventeen- to twenty-two-year-old males would have to volunteer in fiscal 1977; by 1992, one out of every eight would have to be recruited.

Economic Trends

Extrapolations of recent recruiting experience under a range of plausible economic assumptions suggest that difficulties may well develop even before the supply problem discussed above is encountered. Of those men qualified and available, the proportion who volunteer for military service depends on a variety of factors; among the more important are alternative employment and pay opportunities. In other words, as unemployment decreases or as military pay increases fail to keep pace with civilian pay increases, the less likely are individuals to volunteer for military service.[27]

According to economic assumptions underlying the long-term eco-

25. U.S. Bureau of the Census, "Projections of the Population of the United States: 1975 to 2050," *Current Population Reports,* Series P-25, No. 601 (GPO, 1975), pp. 42–59.

26. "Qualified and available" excludes those who *cannot* volunteer (because they are already in the military, institutionalized, or unqualified for mental, physical, or moral reasons) and those who are considered *unlikely* to volunteer (because they are full-time college students or veterans).

27. That these relationships exist is widely accepted; the shape of the curves that represent the relationships, however, is subject to controversy. At issue is the magnitude of the "elasticity factor" (the percentage increase in volunteers that can be expected for a given percentage increase in pay or in unemployment) and the range over which it may be appropriate (the extent to which results based on empirical data can be extrapolated).

Table 6-5. Seventeen- to Twenty-two-year-old Males Qualified and Available for Military Service, Fiscal Years 1977 and 1992
Numbers in thousands

Male population aged seventeen to twenty-two	1977	1992
Total	12,698	10,509
Number who cannot volunteer:		
Institutionalized	190	158
Unqualified	2,252	1,864
Active military	960	960
Number who are not available:		
Full-time students (adjusted for dropouts)	5,403	4,471
Exmilitary	60	60
Qualified and available	3,833	2,996
Recruitment goal as a percentage of those qualified and available	9.5	12.2

Sources: Authors' estimates based on methodology presented in Martin Binkin and John D. Johnston, *All-Volunteer Armed Forces: Progress, Problems, and Prospects*, Report prepared for the Senate Committee on Armed Services, 93:1 (GPO, 1973), appendix A; population figures are from U.S. Bureau of the Census, *Current Population Reports*, Series P-25, No. 601, "Projections of the Population of the United States 1975–2050" (GPO, 1975).

nomic projections made by the Congressional Budget Office in January 1977, anticipated changes in both unemployment and relative pay will work to decrease the number of qualified male volunteers. Embodied in these assumptions are a gradual decline in the male unemployment rate from 7.8 percent in 1977 to 5.1 percent by 1982, while unemployment among males, aged eighteen and nineteen, declines from 17.8 percent to 12.7 percent over the same period. At the same time, while annual military pay increases are to be pegged to raises granted to white-collar civilian employees, these increases—averaging 5.6 percent—are not expected to keep abreast of the average increments accorded blue-collar workers.[28]

With this economic scenario, projected quantitative recruiting goals can be met, but only by sacrificing quality, as shown in table 6-6. The

28. According to CBO, average hourly earnings in manufacturing (excluding overtime)—a broad-based index of blue-collar wages—are expected to increase about 6 percent a year over the period. Concerning the appropriateness of using this index, the CBO explains: "Many youths enter service industries where wage growth may lag behind increases in the manufacturing sector. This would put trends in federal pay in a more favorable light. However, many service workers eventually make careers in the manufacturing sector, and youths considering military service may be more influenced by wage rates in career-type jobs than in temporary jobs." Congressional Budget Office, *The Cost of Defense Manpower: Issues for 1977* (GPO, January 1977), pp. 131–33.

Table 6-6. Comparison of Male Enlistment Requirements and Projected Enlistments of Highly Qualified Males, Fiscal Years 1976–82

Numbers in thousands

Year	Estimated requirements for highly qualified males[a]	Projected enlistments of highly qualified males[b]	
		Number	Percent of requirements for highly qualified males
1976	225	225	100.0
1977	236	220	93.2
1978	236	215	91.1
1979	240	211	87.9
1980	247	203	82.2
1981	241	191	79.3
1982	238	178	74.8

Source: Based on data appearing in Congressional Budget Office, *The Cost of Defense Manpower: Issues for 1977* (GPO, January 1977), pp. 137–38.

a. "Highly qualified" males are defined as those who have completed their high school education and who score above the 30th percentile on standardized tests.

b. Projections based on the economic assumptions discussed in the text, a pay elasticity of 1.00 and unemployment elasticity of 0.45. Thus a 1 percent change in military pay relative to civilian pay and a 2.2 percent change in youth unemployment are each assumed to produce a 1 percent change in enlistments of male high school graduates.

number of "highly qualified" male accessions (defined as those with high school diplomas able to score above the 30th percentile on standardized mental tests) can be expected to decline as alternative employment opportunities expand and as pay increases in the military lag behind those in the private sector. In fact, according to these projections, within five years the services will be able to attract only three-fourths of the highly qualified male recruits that they need. Whether or not national leaders are prepared to accept the decline in standards that these trends suggest is difficult to predict. It is conceivable that pressures could develop to "solve" the problem by granting greater increases in military pay.

There are, of course, many options for improving recruitment, only one of which is to grant across-the-board increases in military pay. To illustrate what might be involved if that tack were followed, it is estimated that just to continue to attract the number of male high school graduates who volunteered in 1976—225,000—the military payroll would have to be close to $6 billion a year greater by 1982 than is currently projected for that year. Over the 1978–82 period, cumulative extra pay costs would be $14 billion.[29] Were the economy to experience an even greater recovery

29. Derived from data provided by the Congressional Budget Office, January 1977.

than is assumed here, prospects would be greater for even larger shortfalls and hence for even higher costs to buy constant "quality."

One alternative is to recruit more women. But this raises the related question: can the military services attract additional women recruits at projected military pay levels?

In truth, very little is known about how many women would enlist in the armed services if they were given the opportunity—or how qualified they would be. Although the Pentagon periodically commissions market research surveys to measure the attitudes of male civilian youths toward military service, virtually none have been done for females. One of the few exceptions was a 1972 study conducted for the Army to measure the interest of women aged eighteen through twenty-four in women's military service, particularly with respect to the Women's Army Corps. Most notable among the results were the following: (1) only 2 percent of all respondents indicated that they were "very familiar" with women's military service whereas 37 percent indicated "no familiarity"; (2) 17 percent described their attitude toward military service as "somewhat favorable" or "very favorable"; (3) only 13 percent reported the same favorable inclination toward the Women's Army Corps in particular; and (4) if faced with the necessity of joining a military service, 37 percent selected the Navy as first choice, 34 percent the Air Force, 17 percent the Army, and 9 percent the Marine Corps.[30]

Nonetheless, prospective women volunteers have actually been turned away, it has been reported, but how many have been rejected and how qualified they are remains speculative. One direct measurement has been made. In fiscal 1974, the armed forces accepted about 48 percent of all women who applied for enlistment. Of 55,000 high school graduates seeking to enlist, about 28,000 (or 51 percent) were accepted; of 9,400 without a high school degree, 2,568 (or 27 percent) were accepted.[31]

Another survey that suggests there might be a wide market for volunteers was made of high school seniors who were administered the Armed Forces Vocational Aptitude Battery (ASVAB) during the 1975–76 school year. Of about 240,000 females responding to an inquiry concerning postgraduate plans, over 11,000 (or 4.7 percent) indicated a prefer-

30. N. W. Ayer and Son, Inc. "A Study of Attitudes Toward Enlistment in the Women's Army Corps" (March 1972; processed), pp. 24, 32, 34.

31. Based on data provided by the Office of the Assistant Secretary of Defense for Manpower and Reserve Affairs, October 1976.

ence for military service.[32] Extrapolated to the total female high school senior group (averaging about 1.5 million over the next five years), close to 75,000 women graduates could be expected to demonstrate a preference for military service, an annual rate that would be sufficient to cover about one-fifth of the total projected requirements for recruits. This number could well become larger if the military services paid greater attention to this potential recruiting pool.

Two factors suggest that large numbers of qualified women might be attracted to military service: first, the supply of female high school graduates of average or above intelligence is barely being tapped by the military and, second, sex discrimination is not a factor in military pay as it is in civilian pay.

There are about 4.1 million eighteen- and nineteen-year-old women in the United States—the age group from which the military prefers to draw most of its recruits. Of this total, an estimated 1 million are single high school graduates not enrolled in college who are in the labor force. About 420,000 of these women could be expected both to score above the 30th percentile on standardized mental tests and to meet current physical standards.[33] The armed forces are currently recruiting some 30,000 women a year, or only about 7 percent of this "quality" group.

There is good reason to believe that an additional number of these women could be attracted to military service under current pay and benefits. As illustrated in chapter 4, a woman recruit can earn far more, on average, than her civilian contemporary in the private sector, and the gap widens the longer she remains in the military service. Despite these differences, just how many additional women would be interested in enlisting is hard to predict. Much would depend on how candidates assessed the non-monetary aspects of military life (working conditions, location, challenge, career opportunity, and the like); on the extent to which the armed forces publicized these opportunities; and on how vigorously the services pursued their recruitment programs. Also important would be the nature

32. Ibid., March 1977.
33. Estimate of number of single female high school graduates in the labor force based on data obtained from Ann McDougall Young, "Students, Graduates, and Dropouts in the Labor Market, October 1975," *Monthly Labor Review*, vol. 99 (June 1976), p. 40. Mental and physical qualification rates based on data appearing in Bernard D. Karpinos, "Recruiting of Women for the Military: Assessment of the Mental and Medical Standards and Their Present and Potential Effects on Recruiting Needs," prepared by the Human Resources Organization for the Directorate for Manpower Research (OASD, Manpower and Reserve Affairs, July 1975; processed).

of the jobs involved; it is possible that the greater the prospect of being assigned to nontraditional jobs, particularly involving combat or sea duty, the more difficult the recruitment of additional women could become. It is also possible that precisely the opposite would occur.

ONE OF THE PENALTIES associated with expanding the role of women in the armed forces, it has long been held, would be an increase in budgetary costs. The cost of a high turnover rate among women, on the one hand, and the necessary additional investment to construct and modify facilities to ensure privacy, on the other, have often been cited.

The foregoing analysis, however, shows not only that the cost differential previously associated with a higher expected personnel turnover rate has been largely eliminated, but also that if one-time costs for separate facilities are incurred, they would be offset, at least in the short run, by annual savings that would result from supporting a smaller dependent population. Furthermore, the larger costs that might accrue because women would be less productive on the job than men for reasons of pregnancy or illness are now more than offset by the greater tendency of men to have disciplinary, drug, and alcoholic problems.

All in all, the force of admittedly scanty evidence is that changes in the sex composition of military services would lead to changes in total costs. Over the long term, however, such differences in costs would probably narrow as more women enter the military services and more of them are employed in nontraditional occupations.

Far and away the most important financial consequence of increasing the proportion of women in the military services—and one that is likely to attract more attention—is the prospect of being able to maintain desired quality standards among volunteers without incurring large increases in the military payroll, using up resources that might otherwise be put to better use elsewhere in the defense establishment or in nondefense activities. Indeed, whether this nation can sustain its armed forces solely by voluntary means could well depend on how effectively the female labor resource is employed.

CHAPTER SEVEN

MILITARY EFFECTIVENESS
AND SEX COMPOSITION

The analysis in chapter 6 indicates that an increase in the proportion of women in the military services could lead to lower financial costs, on the one hand, or could preclude a return to conscription, on the other. Before concluding, however, that women should therefore play a larger role in the U.S. armed forces, the implications for military effectiveness need to be examined.

The problems associated with measuring military effectiveness are well recognized. Even with weapon systems, whose function and purpose may be reasonably pinpointed, it is difficult to measure effectiveness with any confidence. The more labor-intensive the operation becomes, the more difficult it is to identify output and the less quantifiable are the relevant variables. Complex factors such as discipline, leadership, training, societal influence, and group relationships all bear on efficiency. Hence, even when effectiveness analyses are restricted to the performance of men, for which empirical data are available, hard conclusions are rarely attainable. Rigorous conclusions are even more elusive when considering female performance, particularly in nontraditional military jobs for which empirical data are virtually nonexistent. Given these inherent conceptual difficulties and measurement problems, it is not surprising that the arguments on both sides of the issue have been largely ideological.

At one extreme, those who feel that greater reliance on women would weaken the military, point to differences in physical attributes and vocational aptitudes between men and women. Many also believe that women would disrupt the social network considered so important to military organizational effectiveness. And there are some who believe, too, that women would detract from the U.S. military image abroad.

At the other extreme, in the National Organization for Women, the

Committee for Women in the Military, whose motto is: "On Land, on Sea, and in the Air—a Woman's Place is Everywhere," states its position:

Should women go into combat? To us the question is completely irrelevant. We only need to know that there are capable women who want these jobs . . . the question that needs asking is. . . . Does the military have the right to treat their women, regardless of ability, as children who must have their decisions made by others?[1]

This chapter examines three determinants of military effectiveness— individual capabilities, group performance, and image—and how sex differences might affect each. The analysis in this chapter—and throughout most of this study—is primarily confined to enlisted personnel. They constituted 86 percent of the total military population in 1976, and any change in sex composition involves far greater numbers and also, in many instances, very different requirements and types of jobs than it would in the case of officers.

Individual Performance

Job performance depends on such characteristics as mental ability, level of education, job aptitude, physical condition, experience, motivation, adaptability to change, and ability to get along with coworkers. All are to some extent interrelated and their relative importance varies by type of job as well as by experience level within a given occupation.

The military services array jobs by occupational categories, prescribe desired performance levels, and specify minimum standards. For career positions—journeymen and supervisory—experience and job performance evaluations are valuable criteria in selecting appropriate personnel for a given job. For new recruits, however, direct experience ratings are unavailable; thus, educational attainment, standardized test scores, and, to a lesser extent, physical characteristics are used, although each military service employs these indicators in a different way.

Education and Aptitude Differences

The two yardsticks most frequently used to gauge the "quality" of enlistees are level of education and standardized test scores. The military

1. "Testimony by the National Organization for Women before the Defense Advisory Committee for Women in the Services," April 22, 1976 (NOW, 1976; processed).

services place a high premium on completion of high school, not so much because of its relationship to mental achievement—although that is important for some technical courses—but because research over the years has established a consistent inverse relationship between the level of education and the incidence of disciplinary problems.[2] This is not surprising; high school dropouts probably find it even more difficult to adapt, attitudinally and emotionally, to the demanding military environment.

Yet there are no hard-and-fast rules to apply in calculating the proportion of high school graduates required by the services; level of education is not normally included among the specific qualifications identified for enlisted positions. The armed services attempt to attract as many graduates as they can, but because of the labor situation have to settle for some proportion of dropouts. To compensate, however, those who have not completed high school are expected to meet higher standards than graduates in the battery of tests given to prospective recruits. Because the services have stipulated smaller quantitative goals for women, they have been able to be more selective and a far larger proportion of women than men have been high school graduates (see table 7-1).

SELECTION. The services use mental aptitude tests in tandem with level of education as the principal predictors of trainability and, by implication, of job performance. Various composites of a thirteen-part standard test, the Armed Services Vocational Aptitude Battery (ASVAB), qualify prospective volunteers for service. A composite including word knowledge, arithmetic reasoning, and space perception subtests yields a single index of general aptitude for men. The comparable composite for women consists of word knowledge and arithmetic reasoning. On the basis of test scores, examinees are divided into the following groups representing the range from very high military aptitude (Category I) to very low military aptitude (Category V):

Mental Category	Percentile Score
I	93 to 100
II	65 to 92
III	31 to 64
IV	10 to 30
V	9 and below.

2. See, for example, Harold Wool, *The Military Specialist: Skilled Manpower for the Armed Forces* (Johns Hopkins Press, 1968), p. 87; Martin Binkin and John D. Johnston, *All-Volunteer Armed Forces: Progress, Problems, and Prospects,* Report prepared for the Senate Armed Services Committee, 93:1 (GPO, 1973), p. 15; and Martin Binkin and Jeffrey Record, *Where Does the Marine Corps Go from Here?* (Brookings Institution, 1976), p. 63.

Table 7-1. Proportion of Enlisted Recruits with a High School Degree, by Sex, Fiscal Years 1971–76ᵃ

Percent

Recruits	1971	1972	1973	1974	1975	1976
Male	68.3	66.8	65.5	58.1	62.5	66.7
Female	93.9	94.4	95.2	91.7	90.6	91.1
Total	68.9	67.8	66.9	60.8	65.0	68.7

Source: Derived from data provided by the Office of the Assistant Secretary of Defense for Manpower and Reserve Affairs, December 1976.

a. Includes bona fide high school graduates only. Often individuals with a General Educational Development (GED) equivalent are counted as high school graduates.

The test is used principally to differentiate between Mental Category I and II (above average), III (average) and IV–V (below average). Test scores below 10 are disqualifying. Entrants scoring below the 30th percentile are considered by the services to require more training and present greater disciplinary problems than those in the higher groups.

The above general principles apply to all prospective volunteers. But the services use aptitude subtest results in different combinations tailored to their respective needs. To qualify for enlistment in the Army, for instance, male high school graduates are required to score at the 16th percentile or higher on the general aptitude composite and attain a score of 90 or higher on at least one aptitude composite. Males who have not completed high school are required to score at the 31st percentile or higher on the general aptitude composite and attain a score of 90 or higher in two aptitude areas. Women, on the other hand, must possess a high school degree or a GED equivalent, score at the 59th percentile or higher on the general aptitude composite, and attain a score of 90 or higher in one aptitude area.[3]

ASSIGNMENT. The ASVAB consists of the following subtests: word knowledge, arithmetic reasoning, space perception, general information, numerical operations, attention to detail, mathematics knowledge, electronics information, mechanical comprehension, general science, shop information, automotive information, and a classification inventory. Various composites, formed from combinations of these thirteen subtests, are designed to measure training success for clusters of occupations. Minimum scores are established for entry into various programs; for example, to enter training as a carpenter, mason, or electrician, an enlistee must attain a score of at least 90 in the general maintenance aptitude com-

3. Information provided by Department of the Army, April 1977. Scores on aptitude composites are Army Standard Scores, converted from raw scores.

Table 7-2. Aptitude Subtest Components by Army Occupational Area

Occupational Area	Subtest components
Combat	Attention to detail, arithmetic reasoning, space perception, shop information, classification inventory (combat).
Field artillery	General information, arithmetic reasoning, mathematics knowledge, electronics information, classification inventory (attentiveness).
Electronics repair	Arithmetic reasoning, electronics information, mechanical comprehension, shop information, classification inventory (electronic).
Operators and food	General information, automotive information, classification inventory (attentiveness).
General maintenance	Arithmetic reasoning, mechanical comprehension, automotive information, general science.
Motor maintenance	Mathematics knowledge, electronics information, shop information, automotive information, classification inventory (maintenance).
Clerical	Attention to detail, word knowledge, arithmetic reasoning, classification inventory (attentiveness).
Skilled technical	Arithmetic reasoning, mathematics knowledge, general science.
Surveillance/communications	Word knowledge, arithmetic reasoning, space perception, mechanical comprehension.

Source: Department of Defense, "Directions for Scoring Armed Services Vocational Battery" (January 1976; processed).

posite. The formulas and cutoff scores vary by service but the principles are similar.

To illustrate, the occupational areas for which composites are calculated by the Army and the subtests included in each are shown in table 7-2. The subtests associated with industrial occupations are those in which women have traditionally scored lower than men and for which they are considered inherently limited in their suitability for training. This was demonstrated in the results obtained from administering a version of the ASVAB to a large sample of high school students during the 1973–74 school year. As shown in table 7-3, there was a marked difference between the sexes in three composite areas: electronics, general mechanics, and motor mechanics. In each case, males scored much higher. In both the general and clerical composites, however, twelfth-grade students were almost on a par, with the males holding a marginal lead in the general technical and females scoring slightly higher in the clerical area. Under present aptitude standards and measurements, this would imply that only

Table 7-3. Comparative Means and Standard Deviations of ASVAB Raw Scores, Twelfth-Grade Students, by Sex, School Year 1973–74

Subtest or composite	Maximum raw score	Male		Female	
		Mean	Standard deviation	Mean	Standard deviation
Subtests					
Word knowledge	25	14.32	4.88	14.25	4.93
Arithmetic reasoning	25	14.78	5.78	13.03	5.73
Tool knowledge	25	15.25	5.23	6.85	4.15
Space perception	25	14.61	5.74	12.96	5.52
Mechanical comprehension	25	14.71	4.83	10.83	4.41
Shop information	25	15.16	4.64	8.32	4.00
Automotive information	25	14.95	4.76	9.07	3.63
Electronics information	25	14.52	5.05	8.75	4.31
Composites					
General mechanical	75	44.94	12.77	29.60	11.27
Electronics	75	43.75	13.55	28.32	11.20
General technical	50	29.11	9.53	27.29	9.58
Motor mechanics	75	44.61	12.53	28.97	9.50
Clerical	58	29.76	7.58	31.95	7.67

Source: Harry D. Wilfong and others, *Percentile Normative Tables for the Armed Services Vocational Aptitude Battery* (1973–74 School Year Data Base), Technical Research Note 74-3 (Armed Forces Vocational Testing Group, December 1974; processed), p. A2-73.

a small number of women could be expected to qualify for industrial occupations. There are two provisos, however.

First, there might be a "sex bias" in the test instruments that would limit women's occupational choices. According to one researcher, who holds that "sexual bias in testing will become a bigger equal opportunity issue than has racial bias," familiarity with male-oriented subjects is needed to pass at least one-third of the subtests in the ASVAB.[4]

Second, a valid relationship may be found between aptitude test scores and performance in a formal training environment but whether this relates to actual job performance is less clear. Reliable measures of output or productivity and of differential performance in a military environment have yet to be devised.

Until these two issues are resolved, it would be premature to deny to women opportunities to enter nontraditional occupational areas solely on the basis of aptitude scores. Indeed, factors other than aptitude must be considered in predicting or evaluating military effectiveness.

4. Patricia J. Thomas, "Utilization of Enlisted Women in the Military" (San Diego, Calif.: Navy Personnel Research and Development Center, Technical Note, n.d.; processed), p. 24.

Physiological Differences

Obviously, physical strength and endurance are required for effective performance in a variety of military jobs; yet physical standards have been neither well defined nor rigorously applied. The prevailing doctrine has assumed, based on several decades of experience, that individuals capable of meeting minimum medical standards would also be able to acquire a level of physical fitness during basic military training that would qualify them for any job specialty. While physical fitness is not precisely defined, it is usually considered to encompass some combination of strength, endurance, flexibility, balance, speed, agility, and power.

MEDICAL ENTRANCE EXAMS. The examination given to individuals to ascertain whether or not they meet prescribed medical standards includes: (1) clinical examination of the body, (2) laboratory findings, (3) physical measurements (for example, height, weight, blood pressure, and the like), (4) narrative summary of defects and diagnoses, (5) subjective determination of military fitness, (6) identification of any disqualifying defects, and (7) evaluation of the examinee's functional capacity.

The final element—a physician's subjective assessment of an individual's ability to perform military duties—is quantified in terms of a "physical profile," a device once used by all the services but now only by the Army and the Air Force, to communicate an examinee's general physical condition to nonmedical personnel. The profile is intended to serve as an index of overall functional capacity; therefore, the functional capacity of a particular organ or system of the body, rather than any defect per se, is evaluated. The examining physician assigns to six factors, representing the major human functions, a grade on a numerical scale from 1 to 4. The factors now used by the Army are: (1) physical capacity or stamina, (2) upper extremities, (3) lower extremities, (4) hearing and ear defects, (5) eyes, and (6) psychiatric. Together, these factors provide what is commonly called the PULHES profile. The Air Force, as explained below, has recently added a seventh factor.[5]

Grade 1 assigned to a factor signifies a high level of medical fitness; for example, with respect to "physical capacity" it indicates good muscular development with an ability to "perform maximum effort" for indefinite periods. Grade 2 indicates some medical condition or physical defect that may impose certain job limitations; this grade would be assigned to an

5. The change, instituted by the Air Force in *Air Force Regulation 160-43*, Attachment 2, June 21, 1976, is discussed below.

individual who was "able to perform maximum effort over long periods." Grade 3 applies to those with a "moderate" defect; to continue the example, this grade would be given to an individual who is unable to perform maximum effort except for brief or moderate periods. Finally, Grade 4 would indicate that an individual was below minimum standards for enlistment. In assessing physical capacity, the physician considers, in addition to organic defects, such characteristics as age, height, weight, and muscular coordination; until recently, examinees have not been required to demonstrate measurable physical strength and endurance.

Scores assigned to each factor are combined to form a profile serial number. Under current Army personnel procurement standards, two categories of individuals are acceptable for peacetime duty. First, those with a PULHES physical profile serial "111111," signifying no demonstrable anatomical or physiological impairments within established standards, are considered medically fit and can generally be assigned without limitations. The other acceptable group includes those whose profile serial contains a Grade 2 as the lowest designator. For example, slightly limited mobility of joints or muscular weakness are acceptable and the individual is rendered "combat fit," with no significant assignment limitations. In general, Grade 3 or 4 assigned to any factor is disqualifying for initial entrance but is acceptable for someone already in the service.[6]

MEDICAL FINDINGS AND JOB REQUIREMENTS. The relationship between medical examination results and physical requirements associated with specific jobs has varied by service. The Navy and the Marine Corps do not use the PULHES profile for classification purposes and neither service has established physical standards for specific jobs. The Army, on the other hand, associates a profile serial with each specialty. For example, entrance into the infantry career field requires a perfect profile— "111111" (or "picket fence" in military jargon); on the other hand, a "222221" profile is acceptable for, say, a missile electronics repairman. Thus for this latter job the highest score must be attained only in the psychiatric factor whereas some minor defects are acceptable in each of the other factors. Finally, the Air Force, which has taken the lead in experimenting with better measures of physical strength, began to establish more specific standards as early as 1973. Each specialty was classified according to the type of work involved, ranging from "sedentary activity" (lifting 10 pounds maximum) to "very heavy" (lifting objects weighing

6. *Army Regulation 40-501*, Change 31, "Standards of Medical Fitness," May 27, 1976.

a maximum of 100 pounds with frequent lifting or carrying of objects weighing 50 pounds or more).[7] These specifications, however, served mainly as a guide for personnel assignment purposes. The group to which an individual was assigned was not determined by a test of lifting ability but continued to be based on the physician's judgment.

In the absence of realistic physical standards and an appropriate method of measurement, some people undoubtedly were assigned to jobs for which they did not possess sufficient physical strength and endurance. As long as most of the physically demanding skills were closed to women, however, the number of people who could not meet the demands was probably small, being restricted to smaller men who, though able to meet minimum medical standards, might be unable to lift heavy loads. Where this was the case, the men involved were probably assisted by their co-workers or perhaps assigned to lighter duties in the same occupational field; in either event, the philosophy underlying the system was not brought into question—until recently.

ASSESSMENT OF WOMEN'S CAPABILITY. As industrial skills were opened to military women in the early seventies, deficiencies in physical capacity were reported with increasing frequency. In the absence of specific standards, and perhaps in their zeal to project an egalitarian image, the services assigned women to jobs for which many lacked the required physical strength and endurance. Some of the problems that developed were reported by the General Accounting Office, which concluded that a large number of women were assigned to specialties with physical requirements that apparently restricted or precluded their effective performance. According to the GAO:

• Sixty-two of ninety-seven Air Force women assigned to aircraft maintenance duties reported that they did not have sufficient strength to perform many required tasks, such as changing aircraft tires and brakes, removing batteries and crew seats, closing drag chute doors, breaking torque on bolts, and lifting heavy stands.

• The Marine Corps reported that among the women who were being trained to climb telephone poles, most were not able to hoist the necessary equipment, which weighs about 50 pounds.

• Five Army women trained as ammunition storage specialists had been assigned clerical duties in their units because they "physically could

7. Department of the Air Force, *Air Force Manual 39-1*, vol. I, Change 14, Attachment 57, September 5, 1973.

not do the work." At one location, all ammunition had to be moved by hand (rounds weigh 58 pounds and boxes weigh about 120 pounds).

• Army women were also reported to be having difficulty performing the physically demanding duties of ambulance drivers: loading and unloading patients, braking and steering ambulances, and changing wheels and tires.

• Supervisors of Navy women assigned as boatswain's mate on tugboats or other small craft indicated that "women cannot physically do much of the work, which includes lifting and handling sandbags that weigh 100 pounds, paint cans that weigh from 72 to 94 pounds, and boat lines that weigh as much as 7 pounds a foot."[8]

This anecdotal evidence is far from conclusive. But there is no denying, given existing personnel assignment policies, physical examination procedures, and the absence of appropriate standards, that many women (and many small men) could well experience difficulty in effectively performing physically demanding industrial jobs.

MEASUREMENT OF PHYSICAL CAPACITY. Indeed, these concerns prompted the Pentagon to think seriously about establishing more exact physical standards and about developing the techniques that would measure an individual's ability to meet such standards. The Air Force, playing a pioneer role, recently added a seventh item—labeled the "X" factor— to the PULHES profile. The grade assigned to this factor is based on a demonstrated ability to lift a certain weight to a certain height. For example, according to the Air Force, lifting 70 pounds to a height of six feet (Grade 1) indicates an ability to perform "maximum heavy duty" over prolonged periods. Lifting 40 pounds to elbow height (Grade 2) means that an individual can perform sustained moderate duty over prolonged periods. Finally, those able to lift only 20 pounds to elbow height (Grade 3) are considered to be capable of performing standard light duty over normal work periods.[9]

The Air Force has also identified the minimum grade required for each occupation. Of 330 enlisted career fields, 24 require Grade 1, 197 call for Grade 2, and 109, Grade 3. Almost half of 400,000 enlisted jobs are in the "moderate duty" category while only about 63,000, or 16 percent, are deemed to require heavy physical activity, and the remaining 140,000,

8. Comptroller General of the United States, *Job Opportunities for Women in the Military: Progress and Problems* (GAO, 1976), pp. 13–27.

9. Department of the Air Force, *Air Force Manual 160-1*, Change 8, April 17, 1974, and Change 9, Attachment 2, May 2, 1975.

or 35 percent of the total, are in the light physical duty category.[10] During the first year of testing, about 25 percent of the Air Force women were able to lift 70 pounds to a height of six feet—the toughest standard; of the remainder, virtually all could meet the moderate standard—lifting 40 pounds to elbow height.[11]

The Air Force program is an experiment. Whether this single-dimensional, relatively simple measurement is a valid common denominator for predicting physical fitness is still under review. While continuing to observe the results of the Air Force program, the other services apparently have undertaken independent research to compare the physical capacities of men and women and to relate them to classes of jobs. It is worth noting that problems in defining physical requirements and devising valid predictive measures of physical performance are not confined to the armed forces. Wide variations can be observed in the physical agility tests being used by the nation's police departments, ranging from emphasis on brute strength to emphasis on staying power.[12]

THE RELATIVE CAPABILITIES OF MEN AND WOMEN. Appropriate physical standards, valid predictors of physical performance, and the means to measure them have yet to be developed. Until research finds the answers it is difficult to predict how effective women will be in the whole range of industrial skills. What can be concluded at this point, however, is that by most accepted measures men possess greater physical capacity, on average, than women. The reasons for these dissimilarities remain controversial—is the more delicate construction natural or is it a product of a less active culture? But structural and physiological differences between the sexes do indeed exist. The principal differences are to be found in anthropometric, body composition, and the cardiorespiratory factors.

Anthropometric and body composition differences—in size, muscle mass, bone mass, fat distribution, and structure of the elbow joints and pelvis—favor men in strength, explosive power, speed, and throwing and jumping abilities.[13] Researchers at West Point have summarized these

10. Department of the Air Force, *Air Force Manual 39-1,* vol. II, Change 23, Attachment 57, April 26, 1976, and based on data provided by the Department of the Air Force, August 1976.

11. Information provided by the Department of the Air Force, October 1976.

12. See Catherine Higgs Milton and others, *Women in Policing: A Manual* (Police Foundation, 1974), p. 13.

13. The most obvious anthropometric differences are in height and weight: the mean height of 18-year-old males is 69.1 inches compared to 64.1 inches for females of the same age; the mean weights are 151.5 pounds and 126.9 pounds respectively.

differences (see table 7-4). Cardiorespiratory differences—in size of heart and lungs, oxygen content, oxygen uptake (volume of oxygen that can be extracted from inspired air), average hemoglobin content, body temperature, and sweat-gland function—give men an advantage in physical endurance and heat tolerance.

Pregnancy, Menstruation, and Job Performance

How is women's ability to perform military duties affected by pregnancy and menstruation? The question here is not the cost associated with replacing women absent as a result of pregnancy or menstrual problems, but rather how they will affect women's ability to fulfill their duties.

PREGNANCY. Women's unique ability to bear children has been widely used to explain and to justify the division of labor by sex that dominates most industrialized societies. On the assumption that heavy work could have a dangerous effect on mother and child, it has long been thought that women should curtail physical activity during pregnancy. Whether this assumption is valid has not been settled. Drawing on observations in industrialized societies, one researcher concludes that Western attitudes have a cultural rather than biological basis:

... medical data do not support the belief that work is likely to cause problems in pregnancy and childbirth. The real relationship between heavy work before pregnancy and the incidence of miscarriages, still births, etc., is a very indirect one, due to the probability that women from poor homes with inadequate nutrition will both engage in heavy work and be likely to miscarry: what causes the failure is not the work but the poor nutrition in childhood. . . . There are no studies on the relationship between physical exertion and the outcome of pregnancy in societies outside the industrialized West but there is some evidence that physical exercise promotes an easy labour and hence a healthy infant both in our own and in other, dissimilar cultures—confirming the views of those primitive women who believe in work rather than rest as a preparation for childbirth.[14]

Limited evidence suggests that "well-conditioned" women, such as championship-level athletes, who maintain a high degree of physical fitness, have been able to successfully compete until a few days before the onset of labor.[15] What is probably the prevailing attitude of the American

(Data from Department of Health, Education, and Welfare, National Center for Health Statistics.)

14. Ann Oakley, *Sex, Gender, and Society* (Harper and Row, 1972), pp. 136–37.
15. Clayton L. Thomas, "Special Problems of the Female Athlete," in Allan J. Ryan and Fred I. Allman, eds., *Sports Medicine* (Academic Press, 1974), p. 358.

Table 7-4. Characteristics of Adult Anthropometric and Body Composition in Relation to Physical Performance, by Sex

Characteristic	Male	Advantage	Female	Advantage
Height	Taller	Greater lung volume, speed, power	Shorter	Quick rotary
Weight	Heavier	Throwing power	…	…
Muscle mass of total body weight (percent)	Greater	Power, speed, strength	…	…
Body fat of total body weight (percent)	…	…	Greater	Buoyancy
Center of gravity	Higher	Rotary movement	Lower	Balance
Pelvis	Shallower, narrower, heavier	Running speed	…	…
Bi-iliac diameter (hips)	Narrower	Power production	Wider	Stability, childbirth
Bi-acromium diameter (shoulders)	Wider	Weight support production	Narrower	Flexibility
Chest girth	Greater	Thoracic cavity ventilation capacity	…	…
Trunk length	…	…	Relatively longer	Lower center of gravity
Leg length	Relatively longer	Acceleration, speed, power, greater kicking velocity	Relatively shorter	Agility
Elbow joint	Arms parallel from shoulders[a]	Leverage in throwing, supporting weight	…	…

Source: James A. Peterson and others, "Summary Report on Project 60: A Comparison of Two Types of Physical Training Programs in the Performance of 16- to 18-Year-Old Women," United States Military Academy, May 3, 1976 (processed), table I, pp. 119–20.

Note. The same terminology is used in this table as in the source; some detail has been omitted.

a. As opposed to females whose arms form an "x" from shoulders.

medical community, however, has been summed up by one authoritative source: "The type and amount of exercise either indicated or permitted during pregnancy is something each patient, in consultation with her doctor, will have to decide."[16]

Without further research, it is risky to generalize about the relationship between job productivity and pregnancy. It seems safe to conclude, however, that for jobs involving sedentary or light activity, pregnancy would not appreciably affect productivity. In industrial jobs requiring heavier work, on the other hand, some penalty in effectiveness could reasonably be associated with pregnancy. In the extreme environments of ground combat and sea duty, the pregnancy issue has added importance. Pregnant women should probably not be expected to carry out strenuous combat and shipboard duties for as long during the prenatal period as they could under less demanding conditions. Moreover, under these circumstances, pregnant women might be isolated from medical care for prolonged periods.

The prospect of pregnant women in combat gave rise to a sharp, if bizarre, exchange on the floor of the House between two strong-minded adversaries during the debate concerning admission of women to military academies.

According to Congressman Lawrence P. McDonald of Georgia:

It is truly difficult to visualize an effective defense force that included a portion of officers serving while 7, 8, or 9 months pregnant. Going on, can anyone seriously imagine an officer giving a lecture or leading a tank column but requiring a pause to breast-feed her infant? That situation, which might produce a box office triumph in a broadway comedy, has no serious parallel in the real world.[17]

Congresswoman Bella S. Abzug of New York responded:

. . . women were lactating on the frontier of this Nation; and women were lactating on the frontiers of Israel when they fought to establish that homeland. They were lactating during wars throughout the history of this great Nation and the history of the world. Somehow or other that did not stop progress.[18]

MENSTRUATION. Few issues raise the hackles of feminists more than the belabored emphasis placed (usually by men) on the relationship between menstruation and job performance. A survey of Army personnel indicates that military men are particularly apt to attribute women's in-

16. Ibid.
17. *Congressional Record,* daily ed., vol. 121, no. 81 (May 20, 1975), p. H4438.
18. Ibid., p. H4440.

capacity to such factors as menstruation.[19] On the other hand, some women do very little to dispel the notion. In fact, it has been reported (by women) that, in some instances, females tend to exploit the exaggerated importance attached to it by their male supervisors and manage to avoid some duties on the basis of menstrual discomfort.[20]

That some women experience a measure of pain and discomfort at the time of menstruation is widely accepted, but the number affected and the extent of debilitation are open to question. Because of the subjective nature of this symptom complex—called primary dysmenorrhea—the frequency of occurrence reported among women of childbearing age has varied widely; estimates made by various sources range from an incidence of 3 percent to 90 percent.[21] The extent to which job performance is affected among those women who experience these symptoms is also largely unknown. If workdays lost because of menstrual disorders is any guide, the incidence and severity of this condition must have in some instances been overestimated. For example, based on data collected in the 1974 National Health Interview Survey, only one of every twelve women in the labor force could be expected to report a menstrual disorder condition that would entail losing an average of 1.3 days a year; overall, women in the 1974 labor force lost an average of one-tenth of a day per year for menstrual reasons.[22]

The sparse data make it difficult to speculate how the effects would vary with the physical demands of the job: would the "disorder," for instance, be more apt to affect the performance of women in industrialized military occupations? Research results are mixed. An assessment of women's ability to perform complex perceptual-psychomotor tasks during different phases of the menstrual cycle concludes that "there were no performance decrements associated with the menstrual cycle."[23] Based

19. John H. Batts and others, "The Roles of Women in the Army and Their Impact on Military Operations and Organization," U.S. Army War College (May 1975; processed), pp. 35–36.

20. Department of the Navy, internal memorandum, "Subject: Evaluation of Women aboard the U.S.S. *Sanctuary*" (January 3, 1974; processed).

21. Clayton L. Thomas, "Special Problems of the Female Athlete," p. 367. Symptoms include lower abdominal cramps, backaches, feeling of fullness in the abdomen, headache, and, rarely, nausea and vomiting.

22. Data provided by the Department of Health, Education, and Welfare, National Center for Health Statistics, August 1976.

23. A. G. Baisden and R. S. Gibson, "Effects of the Menstrual Cycle on the Performance of Complex Perceptual-Psychomotor Tasks," in *Proceedings of the Nineteenth Annual Meeting of the Human Factors Society, Dallas, Texas, 1975* (Santa Monica, Calif.: the Society, October 1975), p. 145.

on several other studies, however, the performance of female athletes was judged to be "worse" during menstruation by proportions ranging from 17 to 48 percent.[24] Obviously, further research is needed on the relationship between menstruation and physical activity.

Even more controversial is the linking of the menstrual cycle to "social" performance. While the relationship is by no means simple, nor the evidence conclusive one way or the other, the decline in female hormones (estrogen) toward the end of the menstrual cycle appears to be related to a rise in tension and anxiety. Although convicted of far fewer crimes than men, women tend to "commit most of their crimes and other antisocial acts at the low hormonal level (when the hormonal mix most resembles that of a man)."[25]

One researcher estimates that close to one-half of all female admissions to mental hospitals were found to occur during one-fourth of the menstrual cycle—the seven or eight days preceding or during menstruation. Also occurring during this period were 53 percent of attempted suicides by females, 49 percent of crimes committed by women prisoners, and 45 percent of the punishments meted out to schoolgirls.[26] The validity of these results, however, has been disputed on the grounds, first, that the relationship between the menstrual cycle and psychological/emotional states is not only one-way (that is, state of mind and emotion influences the onset of menstruation) and, second, that the various correlates "may not have a great deal of statistical significance."[27] Also needing further examination is the suggestion that social groupings can influence some aspects of the menstrual cycle. One researcher found that college women living in dormitories tended to menstruate at the same time, particularly groups who spend a great deal of time together.[28] While far from conclusive, this concept of "menstrual synchrony" merits attention, particularly as to its possible physical and psychological effect on military

24. James A. Peterson and others, "Project 60: A Comparison of Two Types of Physical Training Programs on the Performance of 16- to 18-Year-Old Women" (United States Military Academy, May 1976; processed), p. 126.

25. Barbara Kirk Cavanaugh, " 'A Little Dearer than His Horse': Legal Stereotypes and the Feminine Personality," *Harvard Civil Rights–Civil Liberties Law Review*, vol. 6 (March 1971), p. 270.

26. Based on research conducted by Katherina Dalton, University of London, as reported by Lionel Tiger, "Male Dominance? Yes, Alas. A Sexist Plot? No." *New York Times Magazine* (October 25, 1970), p. 132.

27. Ann Oakley, *Sex, Gender, and Society*, p. 45.

28. Martha K. McClintock, "Menstrual Synchrony and Suppression," *Nature*, vol. 229 (January 22, 1971), pp. 244–45.

units composed of a high proportion of women in continuous close contact.

Also fueling the controversy is an emerging body of research on the issue of whether men undergo cyclic emotional variation. At least one study hypothesizes that men, too, have a monthly temperature cycle and may periodically suffer some of the same psychological and emotional symptoms associated with the female menstrual cycle. Research is in its very early stages and, according to one prominent physiologist, the "data must be amplified many times before one feels safe in saying it's a universal phenomenon."[29]

In sum, because the relationships are inadequately researched and poorly understood, predictions concerning the effects of pregnancy or menstruation on job performance remain largely speculative.

Emotional Differences

Few would deny that men and women are temperamentally different. Does this mean that women would not perform as well as men under stress? If such a speculation is true, how effective would women be in nontraditional jobs, particularly combat? Stereotypical differences in personality have been suggested by such devices as the Masculinity-Femininity test and the Rorschach ink-blot tests. Some of the main characteristics of the personality dichotomy have been summarized:

> In word association, females tend to choose words for articles of dress, personal adornment, colors, aesthetic appraisal, domestic things and happenings, and words indicating a "kind" and "sympathetic" social orientation. Conversely, the male preference is for words describing outdoor phenomena, activity and adventure, science and machinery, political, business and commercial enterprise . . . the key masculine quality is "the aggressive, adventurous, enterprising, outwardly directed disposition: the tendency to pugnacity and self-assertiveness." The outstanding feminine traits are "the actively sympathetic, the inwardly directed disposition: the maternal impulse and the tender feelings; concern with domestic affairs."[30]

Deep-rooted resistance to the notion of women in combat, then, is a natural consequence of the juxtaposition of personality norms, on the

29. Estelle Ramey, Georgetown University, commenting on a study by the Australian researcher, Margaret Henderson (quoted in the *Washington Star-News,* September 12, 1976).

30. Ann Oakley, *Sex, Gender, and Society,* pp. 49–50.

one side, and descriptions of combat and its demands, on the other. According to one professional observer:

In the combat situation, the soldier not only faces the imminent danger of loss of life and, more frightening for most, limb, but also witnesses combat wounds and deaths suffered by "buddies." Moreover, there are the routine physical stresses of combat existence: the weight of the pack, tasteless food, diarrhea, lack of water, leeches, mosquitos, rain, torrid heat, mud, and loss of sleep. In an actual firefight with the enemy, the scene is generally one of utmost chaos and confusion.[31]

The relative aggressiveness of men and women has also been cited as a factor in assessing the possible combative skills of women. While anthropologists tend to agree that men are more aggressive, they disagree on the etiology: are the differences cultural or biological? One of the most widely known commentators in her field concluded:

The historical and comparative material at least suggests that it may be highly undesirable to permit women, trained to inhibit aggressive behavior, to take part in offensive warfare. Defensive warfare, on the other hand, does not have the same disadvantages, as it invokes the biological basis of defense of the nest and the young.[32]

Group Performance

Thus far the discussion of comparative effectiveness of men and women in military occupations has centered on the capabilities of the individual. In discussing the effectiveness of military units—particularly combat units or naval vessels, the importance of group relationships cannot be overlooked. Indeed, the implications of introducing women into military units previously dominated by men raises a new set of issues; in addition to individual physical and aptitude considerations, it is necessary to consider group behavior.

At the outset, it is important to point out that an understanding of the behavior and performance of *men* in groups, particularly under combat or sea-duty conditions, is far from complete; an understanding of the behavior and performance of *women* under these conditions is very small;

31. Charles C. Moskos, Jr., *The American Enlisted Man: The Rank and File in Today's Military* (Russell Sage Foundation, 1970), p. 141.

32. Margaret Mead, "A National Service System as a Solution to a Variety of National Problems," in Sol Tax, ed., *The Draft: A Handbook of Facts and Alternatives* (University of Chicago Press, 1967), p. 108.

and precious little is known about the effects of combining men and women.[33]

Two contrasting schools of thought are discussed here. One implies that the integration of women into combat units or aboard naval vessels could pose significant problems; the other suggests less dire consequences.

Male-bonding

The first subscribes to the hypothesis that men tend to draw together in social groups from which women are excluded.[34] This is particularly true, it is argued, in matters involving the control of interferences to social order, such as politics, war, and police work. Thus it is held:

(1) that defence and maintaining the social order are clearly crucial to the persistence of human social systems; (2) that these behaviors are typically undertaken by males, usually without female full colleagues . . . (3) that on all occasions defined by a community as vitally important and during which strong emotion is experienced by community members aware of the overall situation a male or males will assume the most significant roles.[35]

This hypothesis implies that in matters pertaining to organized agression "not only will males and females reject other females as potential leaders and defenders, but that males will reject females as colleagues."[36]

If accurate, this portrayal of an antifemale pattern could affect combat units. Military organizations, particularly those elite units closely associated with a machismo image (such as airborne and ranger units or warships), tend to attract individuals because of that image. The type of volunteer might change if women were introduced, perhaps disrupting group cohesion and, hence, combat effectiveness. This view is upheld by the Department of the Navy:

33. For discussion of contemporary theories of combat behavior, see Samuel A. Stouffer and others, *The American Soldier: Combat and Its Aftermath* (Princeton University Press, 1949), vol. II; Roger W. Little, "Buddy Relations and Combat Performance," in Morris Janowitz, ed., *The New Military: Changing Patterns of Organization* (Russell Sage Foundation, 1964), pp. 195–223; and Charles C. Moskos, Jr., *The American Enlisted Man.*

34. The principal proponent of this view, Lionel Tiger, suggests that "there is a biological program that results in a 'bonding' between males which is important for politics as the program of male-female bonding is for reproduction." See Lionel Tiger, "Male Dominance? Yes, Alas. A Sexist Plot? No," p. 126.

35. Lionel Tiger, *Men in Groups* (London: Thomas Nelson and Sons, 1969), pp. 84–85.

36. Ibid., p. 85.

Since the inception of the Continental Navy, later the U.S. Navy, traditional male domination of warfare and seafaring has continued. Only recently has there been pressure for change. The naval profession—specifically the business of going to sea—has been advertised as, and accepted as, a closed club for men.

The present male-dominated, sea-going facet of Navy life is one that is understood and accepted by the country and the men in the Navy. Men join the Navy for many different reasons; however, a certain portion join and remain in the Navy because they enjoy being in a job which has been historically associated with fellowship among men in a difficult and dangerous endeavor. Changing the fabric of the Navy by integrating women into àll combat roles might well reduce the attractions of the Navy to this segment of mankind, as well as to some of those men who might, in the future, join the Navy and make it a career.[37]

It is becoming increasingly difficult, however, to reconcile this hypothesis with the mounting evidence of women's prominent role in terrorist and guerrilla groups, in which strong patterns of male-bonding would be expected to exist. Women have been conspicuous in some of the more notorious groups: the Symbionese Liberation Army (SLA), the Popular Front for the Liberation of Palestine (PFLP), the Croation Nationalists (USTASHI), and the Baader-Meinhof Gang.

Individuation: An Alternate View

Other analysts of combat behavior attach less importance to the influence of social networks—called "primary" groups in the idiom of the sociologist.[38] The social cohesiveness observed at the squad and platoon level in World War II and the two-man "buddy" relationship in the Korean War has given way to an individualistic ethos.[39]

According to this view, based in part on the more rapid turnover of personnel in combat units during the Korean and Vietnam Wars and in part on the value commitments of combat soldiers to the American social

37. Appraisal provided by Admiral Worth Bagley, then Vice Chief of Naval Operations, *Hearings on H.R. 9832 to Eliminate Discrimination Based on Sex with Respect to the Appointment and Admission of Persons to the Service Academies,* Hearings before the House Armed Services Committee, 93:2 (GPO, 1975), p. 120.

38. "By primary groups, sociologists mean those small social groupings in which social behavior is governed by intimate face-to-face relations." See Morris Janowitz, *Sociology and the Military Establishment* (Russell Sage Foundation; 1959), p. 64.

39. Charles C. Moskos, Jr., *The American Enlisted Man,* pp. 143–46.

system, individual self-interest is paramount; the ultimate standard of combat behavior rests on each individual's fight for survival.[40]

This school holds that the masculine ethic so long associated with combat behavior may be exaggerated. While "masculinity" and "physical toughness" have motivated individuals to enter combat, their importance has receded "once the life-and-death facts of warfare are confronted."[41]

This interpretation of the determinants of behavior in combat suggests that the introduction of women into fighting organizations or seagoing units would have less disruptive effects on solidarity than are indicated by a stricter interpretation of primary group theory, particularly when male-bonding is one of the dominant cohesive forces in the primary group.

Extent of Integration and Its Effect on Group Performance

It may well turn out that only small numbers of qualified women will be interested in nontraditional military duty. In that event, it would be important to consider the possibility, indicated by research, that the performance of mixed sex groups may be sensitive to the composition of the mix. Research suggests that as long as women are in the minority, men will continue to view them according to preconceived stereotypes and to fulfill their own need to project the male image. This would tend to isolate women, keep the male group in conflict with them, and thus reduce overall group productivity.[42]

Also meriting attention are the possible effects of social alliances and sexual pairings on unit performance. Integration studies at Yale and Princeton Universities found generally that, while the ideal mix was not surprisingly half and half, social problems were less likely to develop when the ratio of men to women was lower than three to one. Above that threshold, according to the researchers, some women tended to assume a "superwoman" role and to make more male friends than they normally would, while the men tended to socially reject them as inferior.[43]

40. Ibid., p. 145.
41. Ibid., pp. 154–55.
42. For example, see Ross A. Webber, "Perceptions and Behaviors in Mixed Sex Work Teams," *Industrial Relations,* vol. 15 (May 1976), and Diane N. Ruble and E. Tory Higgins, "Effects of Group Sex Composition on Self-Presentation and Sex Typing," *Journal of Social Issues,* vol. 32, no. 3 (1976), pp. 125–32.
43. James H. Thomas and Dirk C. Prather, "Integration of Females into a Previously All-Male Institution," *Proceedings of the Fifth Symposium on Psychology in the Air Force* (United States Air Force Academy, Department of Behavioral Sciences and Leadership, April 1976), pp. 100–01.

The U.S.S. Sanctuary *and Other Experiments*

U.S. armed forces have some, if sparse, empirical data on the effect of introducing women into male-dominated groups.

THE "SANCTUARY" EXPERIENCE. In 1972, by the direction of Admiral Elmo R. Zumwalt, erstwhile chief of naval operations, the Navy undertook a test program designed to evaluate the assignment of a limited number of women to the ship's company of the U.S.S. *Sanctuary,* the last of the Navy's hospital ships.

All told, 53 enlisted women, constituting about 12.5 percent of the total enlisted complement, were assigned to jobs in each of the ship's seven departments: hospital, 21; deck, 9; supply, 4; operations, 3; resale, 10; administration, 5; and engineering, 1.[44]

After thirteen months in an integrated configuration, an evaluation made by the ship's commanding officer included the following main conclusions:

• "Women are capable and may serve onboard the *Sanctuary,* under the present administrative conditions, in perpetuity."

• "Women can perform every shipboard function with equal ease, expertise, and dedication as men do. (No experience available to judge applicability to engineering rates)."[45]

Speculation centered on the effect of sex integration on moral standards. Here, the report speaks for itself:

Soon after enlisted women reported onboard, they found themselves courted by the young sailors. The period of inactivity at HPNSY [Hunters Point Naval Shipyard, San Francisco, California] created the opportunity for constant offship socializing. Cynics and those critical to the assignment of women onboard lost no opportunity to point out that the Navy is providing three-squares, shelter, a woman, and money to enjoy it. Such branding, however, would be unjust to the greatest majority of men and women assigned to *Sanctuary* who have constantly exhibited high moral standards; it would also be unfair to those few who through their good fortune of being assigned to the same command found true affection, have gotten married or are engaged to be married.

The 12-day at sea period, from 1–12 October 1973, enroute from Alameda, California to Buenaventura, Colombia gave rise to many interesting observa-

44. "Evaluation of Women Aboard the U.S.S. *Sanctuary*" (Memorandum from the Commanding Officer, U.S.S. *Sanctuary* [AH-17] to Chief of Naval Personnel, November 19, 1973), p. 15-1.

45. Ibid.

tions. Fair weather and smooth seas prevailed throughout the transit. Warm subtropical temperatures necessitated shifting to tropical uniforms and T-shirts and many recreational activities were carried out on the weather decks after working hours and during holiday routine. Then all of a sudden, public display of affection that once was very discreet and non-existent, crept in. This had a demoralizing effect on both men and women and most particularly on the senior petty officers. The situation was becoming serious and was definitely detrimental to the good order and discipline of the ship's company. At that time, the command issued a statement of administrative policy to all hands making public and open display of affection a violation and making those who failed to conform liable for NJP [non-judicial punishment] for acts or activities contrary to the good order and discipline of the naval service. It appears that this has worked. At present not as much as hand-holding can be seen onboard.[46]

With respect to morale, the report indicated that by and large the enlisted men favored the presence of women on board since "they have someone of the other sex to talk to, affording at least a semblance of normal social relations."[47]

One of the most important, and most widely publicized, problems was the concern expressed by the wives of shipboard personnel of the heightened possibility of sexual involvement between their husbands and Navy women living in close proximity for prolonged periods at sea. According to the report, "the ship undertook a vigorous program of informative meetings with enlisted wives onboard and held a family cruise prior to departure for Colombia," and concluded that "gradually wives have realized that their fears were unfounded and they generally dissipated."[48]

Subsequent research indicates, however, that about one-third of the wives of naval personnel strongly oppose shipboard assignments for women and about 11 percent have felt strongly enough about it to urge their husbands to leave the Navy.[49] Although these results were based on limited data, this situation bears watching and warrants additional research since the satisfaction of wives with Navy life has been shown to have an important influence on their husbands' decision concerning a naval career.

The *Sanctuary* experiment is encouraging on the whole but there are two points to remember in applying it to the future prospects of integra-

46. Ibid., p. 13-2.
47. Ibid., p. 13-1.
48. Ibid., p. 13-2.
49. Patricia J. Thomas and Kathleen P. Durning, "The Military Woman and the Navy Wife," Paper presented at the Eighty-fourth Annual Convention of the Ameri-

tion on naval vessels. First, many key personnel selected for this experimental project underwent stricter screening and thus may not have represented a cross-section of naval personnel; and second, the ship was actually under way for a period of only forty-two out of a total of close to 400 days.[50] Viewed in a proper context, however, this experiment identified many of the problems that should be anticipated and pointed the direction of future research.

OTHER EXPERIMENTS. Also worth noting are two 1976 experimental Army programs. First, a test (called MAX-WAC) was initiated in July to assess the effects of varying the percentage of female soldiers assigned to representative types of units (excluding those that operate forward of the brigade rear boundary) on the capability of a unit to perform its mission. This test is scheduled to be completed in June 1977.[51]

Second, a test program was established to evaluate the relative capabilities of male and female recruits to meet the standards employed in the basic combat training previously given only to males. The usual women's basic training program was modified to include individual tactical techniques, hand grenade instruction, more strenuous physical training, and familiarization courses for a greater variety of weapons. Two training battalions, each consisting of two companies of men and two companies of women, were administered a virtually identical training program. Altogether, 875 male and 823 female recruits entered the course; 87.3 percent of the males and 85.3 percent of the females completed it. Among the major findings were, first, that "female graduates met the standard in every area except the Physical Readiness Training Program, and that those events can be modified for the women without changing the content of the training or reducing the value of training received," and, second, that the course "with modifications is an acceptable initial entry program for female accessions."[52]

---

can Psychological Association, Washington, D.C. (San Diego, Calif.: Navy Personnel Research and Development Center, September 1976; processed).

50. "Evaluation of Women Aboard the U.S.S. *Sanctuary*," pp. 1-1 to 1-8.

51. Department of the Army, "Outline Test Plan—Women Content in Units (MAX-WAC)," FO 048 (May 21, 1976; processed).

52. U.S. Army Military Police School Training Center, "Basic Initial Entry Training (BIET)—Test Report" (December 30, 1976; processed), pp. 1-1 to 1-5, 3-7. In April 1977 the Army announced that, commencing in October 1978, a common basic training course would be given to male and female recruits. See TRADOC News Service, Release No. 30-77 (U.S. Army Training and Doctrine Command, April 22, 1977; processed).

Foreign Experience

To some extent, the experiences of other nations should contribute to a better understanding of the issues involved here. Of particular interest would be data on the two instances of relatively widespread use of women in war, including the role of combatants: Soviet women during World War II and Israeli women during the 1948 Arab-Israeli conflict over the future of Palestine. Apart from the scant information recounted in chapter 2 and the appendix, however, there is little else available in the unclassified literature. If U.S. intelligence sources have access to additional information, research should be directed toward what can be learned about how women reacted under fire, how the populace reacted to female casualties, how males reacted to women in their units, and the impact of male-female relationships upon the combat effectiveness of the units. Caution would have to be exercised both in assessing the objectivity of the sources and in drawing parallels from wartime situations (in which both nations found themselves in an underdog role) for contemporary U.S. policies on the sex composition of peacetime forces.

Image Abroad

In many respects, the effectiveness of armed forces should be measured as much in terms of an ability to deter military adventures by an enemy as in terms of an ability to defeat him. What signal would be conveyed by a greater reliance on women in the military? Would potential adversaries perceive a U.S. military force composed of a larger proportion of women as more, or less, powerful? Much would depend on the nation, its societal views, and its experience with women in its own military establishment. In any event, an increase in the number of women in the U.S. armed forces would probably attract little attention anywhere unless it resulted in a dramatic shift in total sex composition or unless it was accompanied by an unprecedented integration of women into U.S. fighting units.

The Soviet Union's perceptions of an increase in the role of women in the U.S. armed forces are likely to be shaped largely by the limited status now accorded to Russian women, both in their military establishment and in their society as a whole (see the appendix). Although many women were pressed into service when the Soviet Union was attacked in World War II, they have since played a relatively minor part in the military forces. According to recent intelligence estimates, the Soviet military establishment, totaling over 4 million, employs only about 10,000 women.[53] This suggests that the Kremlin might be inclined to view an expanded role for women in the U.S. armed forces, particularly in an unprecedented combat role, as a sign of weakness induced by recruiting difficulties. The Russians would be unlikely to understand, much less appreciate, the equal rights rationale that might underlie women's greater participation.

On the other hand, the People's Republic of China, whose Communist leadership has always viewed women's liberation as "part of the struggle against feudalism, capitalism, and imperialism,"[54] would no doubt comprehend and perhaps sympathize with this view. Women have participated actively in China's revolutionary movements for the past 150 years; in fact, women reportedly fought alongside men in the T'ai P'ing Rebellion of 1851 and were conspicuous in other actions "against the imperial dynasties, against the Chinese war lords, against the Japanese invaders, against western imperialist-concessionaires, and later against the nationalist forces of Chiang Kai-shek."[55]

Reactions among the Arab nations are even more difficult to predict since the literature on the sociology of contemporary Arab cultures is so limited. Moreover, it is risky to generalize because of vast differences among the various religious confessions involved; attitudes toward women could well run the gamut of possibilities. Many Arab societies appear to be undergoing a sexual revolution but, according to one observer, the pace of change is "so slow that generations must pass before sexual equality is recognized in the Western sense."[56]

Virtually no information is available on the sex composition of Arab military forces. Educated speculation, however, suggests that some of the more progressive Arab nations, following the Israeli model, may have begun to train women for military duty. This is not surprising since recent

53. U.S. Defense Intelligence Agency, "Women in the Soviet Armed Forces," DDI-1100-109-76 (March 1976; processed), p. 5.

54. Jane C. Record and Wilson Record, "Sex Roles and the State: A Comparison of the Chinese and American Appearances," Paper presented to the American Sociological Association, San Francisco, California (August 1975; processed), p. 3.

55. Ibid., pp. 13-14; see also Jane C. Record and Wilson Record, "Totalist and Pluralist Views of Women's Liberation: Some Reflections on the Chinese and American Settings," *Social Problems*, vol. 23 (April 1976), pp. 402–14.

56. John Laffin, *The Arab Mind Considered* (Taplinger, 1975), p. 98.

Arab-Israeli conflicts have promoted in that part of the world a greater awareness that modern warfare relies more on technology than on muscle. Indeed, in stark contrast to the American public's image of ground combat—infantrymen slogging through the jungles of Vietnam—Arabs and Israelis are more likely to perceive it as the engagement of mechanized formations in which brain is more important than brawn.

Conclusions

The effectiveness of military forces depends largely on individual capabilities, group performance, and the public image abroad. As the discussion above indicates, a healthy measure of uncertainty remains about how greater female participation would affect all three. Until appropriate yardsticks are developed for each of them, predictions are highly speculative.

Obviously there are many military jobs that the average woman could do at least as effectively as the average man; on the other hand, there are many jobs that, at this stage of cultural development, she could not do as effectively. How large each group of jobs is can be roughly approximated.

First, in occupations in which women have traditionally been employed, there is little question that they can perform *at least* on a par with men. Included are a wide range of technical and administrative positions for which the principal requirements are general intelligence and academic ability, characteristics that women, on average, are as likely to possess as men. In these occupations, which are analogous to white-collar jobs in the civilian sector, physical strength is relatively unimportant. For example, jobs in administration, health care, communications, intelligence, and other technical occupations (photography, mapping, weather) are largely sedentary or, at most, involve light work.[57] Some 540,000 enlisted jobs, or about one out of every three, are in this category; about 11 percent are now filled by women. The distribution by service is shown in table 7-5. By contrast, of approximately 18 million jobs in similar categories in the civilian sector, some 10 million, about 55 percent, are held

---

57. This categorization is an attempt to simplify complex and poorly defined relationships and it has inherent limitations. Obviously, there are some jobs in communications and intelligence that are anything but white-collar. On the other hand, there are jobs in the blue-collar category that do not require heavy labor.

Table 7-5. Distribution of Enlisted White-Collar Jobs in the Armed Forces, by Military Service, June 1976

Occupational category	Army	Navy	Marine Corps	Air Force	Total
Communications and intelligence	58,078	39,563	12,590	36,474	146,705
Medical and dental	30,543	27,586	—	19,845	77,974
Other technical	12,587	5,679	2,925	18,075	39,266
Administrative	107,332	43,535	24,569	102,040	277,476
White-collar jobs, total	**208,540**	**116,363**	**40,084**	**176,434**	**541,421**
Percent of total enlisted jobs	35.7	32.1	27.6	39.7	35.3

Source: Data provided by the Office of the Assistant Secretary of Defense for Manpower and Reserve Affairs, January 1977.

by women.[58] With few exceptions, women could be at least as effective in these jobs as men.

How effective women would be in the remaining jobs is less clear and in need of further study. Included are those positions roughly comparable to blue-collar jobs in the private sector: equipment repair, crafts (metalworker, machinist, carpenter), and service and supply handlers. Along with the so-called combat skills, these positions require physical capabilities and aptitudes now more often found in males than in females. The distribution of these jobs is shown in table 7-6. Although most are now "open" to women (the combat skills are the principal exception), approximately 17,000, or only about 1.7 percent of the blue-collar jobs, are currently filled by women. In contrast, close to 21 percent of comparable civilian jobs have a female incumbent.[59]

All positions on this roster do not require extraordinary strength or a traditionally masculine aptitude and, among the jobs that do, some proportion of the female population could be expected to meet the requirements. Until physical and aptitude standards and measurements are

58. Based on unpublished data provided by the U.S. Bureau of the Census, November 1976. The figures include year-round, full-time workers in two major classes of occupations: professional, technical, and kindred (salaried only); and clerical and kindred.

59. Ibid. The following categories are considered to be blue-collar: craft and kindred workers; operatives; laborers, except those on farms; and service workers, except those in private households. The last category accounts for close to half of the women counted as blue-collar workers. Most of these women are in food service jobs. If the service worker category is omitted, women fill about 13 percent of civilian blue-collar jobs.

Table 7-6. Distribution of Enlisted Blue-Collar Jobs in the Armed Forces, by Military Service, June 1976

Occupational category	Army	Navy	Marine Corps	Air Force	Total
Infantry, gun crews, and seamanship	165,697	16,249	43,103	4,785	229,834
Electronic equipment repairmen	31,852	58,690	7,647	66,812	165,001
Electrical/mechanical equipment repairmen	89,109	119,088	26,981	105,599	340,777
Craftsmen	18,741	27,024	4,049	25,043	74,857
Service and supply handlers	70,287	24,635	23,136	65,681	183,739
Blue-collar jobs, total	**375,686**	**245,686**	**104,916**	**267,920**	**994,208**
Percent of total enlisted jobs	64.3	67.9	72.4	60.3	64.7

Source: Same as table 7-5.

well defined and until physical and aptitude characteristics of the female population are better understood, a comparative effectiveness analysis is not possible.

Skills still closed to women—those involving combat—warrant special attention. Although women are not barred from these specialties solely because of physical and aptitude considerations, these factors need to be considered. Among the most physically demanding tasks in the armed forces are those involved with the direct labor of war—those performed by infantrymen, tank crews, artillerymen, and fighting ships' personnel. For example, "straight-legged" infantrymen, whose principal means of mobility on the battlefield is by foot, are required to lift and carry equipment exceeding one-quarter of their own weight over long distances, a task seemingly too arduous for the vast majority of American women. Perhaps less demanding of physical endurance, successful performance in the other combat specialties depends more on brute strength. Tank crews load heavy ammunition in a cramped environment and perform heavy maintenance under field conditions. Artillery crews are similarly called upon to lift heavy ammunition rounds, and ship crews, regardless of their specialties, are expected under emergency conditions to perform a wide range of physically demanding tasks, some of which may not be directly related to their job. Moreover, the effects of integration on group performance in combat—about which little is known—ought also to be considered.

FINALLY, SOME WOMEN will be at least as capable as some men to do the most demanding military tasks, including combat. Feminists argue, therefore, that all remaining barriers should be removed, all occupational opportunities should be open equally to men and women, and the recruitment, classification, and assignment process should deal with individual attributes and select the most qualified irrespective of sex. The problem with this reasoning is that, as matters now stand, standards and predictors of selection, classification, and assignment are not sufficiently refined to assess with any confidence how any individual or group of individuals will perform military functions.

This is not to condone the existing system, which permits blanket prohibitions based on sex. It says, however, that the removal of these prohibitions should be preceded by a resolution of the fundamental issues discussed in this chapter. To do otherwise could court undue risk to U.S. national security interests.

CHAPTER EIGHT

WOMEN AND THE MILITARY: TOWARD OPTIMUM UTILIZATION

Sooner or later this nation will have to confront the controversial issue of whether the laws and policies that circumscribe the role and number of women in the armed forces should be changed and, if so, how. The issue is important; its resolution could have significant social, economic, and military implications.

The purpose of this study has been to provide the bases and rationale for possible change; to present all sides of the issues; and, below, to recommend concrete and practical proposals for immediate action and suggest areas where further investigation and research are needed.

The extremes—status quo or full equality—are not considered appropriate. To maintain present laws and policies denies women their rights and denies the country a pool of competent workers who might be willing to serve in the armed forces. The consequences of granting full equality, on the other hand, have not yet been fully explored and cannot be adequately assessed either for military effectiveness or for society as a whole.

Although current restrictions on female participation are discriminatory in principle, it would be imprudent to eliminate them without first obtaining a clearer indication of the relative capabilities of integrated combat forces and without determining how interested women are in combat service. On the other hand, the analysis indicates that the goals set by the services for women's participation do not appear to represent maximum effort to eliminate discrimination, even within current combat restrictions. This suggests a twofold approach for moving toward an optimum utilization of women in the armed forces.

The first would call for a reassessment of the policies now used to shape the sex composition of the services. This could be done fairly soon and would not require changes in legislation. However, with the exception of the Air Force, this measure could be expected to yield only modest changes; to go further would require a resolution of the more fundamental combat issue. Thus the second step would call for narrowing, if not resolving, the uncertainties that now plague the combat question. An experimental program would have to be established in each service to test the feasibility of integrating women in combat units before modifying existing arrangements that restrict women from such duty. The planning, development, and administration of such an experiment could be initiated immediately, but it would take some years to evaluate the results and decide on what action to take.

Assessing Current Rationales

Each of the armed services applies somewhat different methods with varying degrees of sophistication in developing their goals for women's participation, but their general approach is somewhat similar. First, they identify those positions that women cannot fill because of legislative restrictions or their interpretation of the intent of those restrictions; second, they set aside additional billets for men to allow them equal assignment and career development opportunities; and finally, a "management" adjustment is made to account for such items as lack of adequate accommodation and a balanced female distribution by grade and occupation.

The results, discussed in chapter 3, are summarized in table 8-1. Among the more striking features are the relatively large proportion (61 percent) of "restricted" jobs in the Army, the high proportion of Army and Navy billets set aside for assignment rotation and career development (about 30 and 34 percent, respectively), and the relatively low proportion (13 percent) of "open" (sex-neutral) positions that, by Air Force projections, women will occupy. By any reckoning, the goals for the female work force appear inordinately small. But, given the many factors involved, the complicated relationships between them, and the lack of publicly available data, how much the goals are understated in table 8-1 can only be roughly approximated.

Women in the Army

In the absence of specific legislative restraints, Army policies on the assignment of women have been shaped by "the will of the American people." The Army's interpretation implies that (1) no women engage in

Table 8-1. Comparison of Military Enlisted Job Opportunities, by Sex.[a]
Thousands

Service	Total number of enlisted positions	Enlisted positions for males only		"Open" positions	Goals for female participation[d]
		Restricted[b]	Reserved[c]		
Army	676.0	415.0	206.0	55.0	50.4
Navy	464.0	287.0	153.0	24.0	21.1
Marine Corps	171.0	128.0	34.5	8.5	6.7
Air Force	477.0	31.0	83.0	363.0	48.2
Department of Defense total	1,788.0	861.0	476.5	450.5	126.4

Source: Authors' estimates.
a. Totals include "pipeline" personnel (transients, students, and the like).
b. Restricted positions are those that are closed to women because of statutory restrictions or a particular service's interpretation of those restrictions.
c. Reserved positions are those that might otherwise be available to women but that are reserved for men for assignment rotation, career development, housing limitations, or other management purposes.
d. Service goals for fiscal 1982, as projected in Office of the Assistant Secretary of Defense for Manpower and Reserve Affairs, "Use of Women in the Military," background study (OASD, Manpower and Reserve Affairs, May 1977; processed). As discussed in chapter 3, the figures for the Navy and the Air Force are tentative and subject to revision.

combat-related occupations; (2) no women are assigned to direct combat units, and (3) limits are set on the extent to which women can participate in all other units, the limits depending on how near units are operating to the "front line." Together these constraints limit the number of Army positions that women could occupy to about 261,000, a figure that is further reduced to 55,000 by rotation, career development, and other "management" considerations (see chapter 3).

While, under present conditions, it is difficult to argue against the exclusion of women from combat jobs, the restriction against assigning women to any unit expected to operate in the brigade area is contestable, and the logic of setting graduated limitations on their assignment to all other units far from persuasive.

According to the Army, the relatively low proportion of females permitted in units operating behind the brigade area is an attempt to keep women out of contact with the enemy and, because of unusual physical demands, out of units that must move frequently. For example, the Army restricts to 10 percent the proportion of women in units that are expected to operate in the division area (typically located between thirty and fifty-five kilometers from the front lines). The possibility of intense combat activity at that distance from the front is relatively small; and, in any event, why is the risk that females constitute 10 percent of the casualties deemed acceptable, and not, say, 30 or 40 percent?

Before 1974 the assignment of enlisted women was at the discretion of the respective Army commanders so that, in fact, some women did perform duties in many units operating within the brigade area.[1] In 1974, however, the regulation was changed to prohibit assignment to such units, an action that might possibly have been tied to the congressional debate over whether or not to admit women to the nation's military academies. The combat issue was one of the Army's principal arguments against women at West Point: an argument considerably weakened if female soldiers were already assigned to units expected to operate near the front.[2] Nonetheless, despite the changed regulation, the Army still continues to assign women to jobs in which it is very likely that they will be called upon to operate forward of the brigade rear boundary (for example, mobile maintenance specialists at the division level). It must be remembered that women had been routinely deployed forward during World War II; Wacs following the Fifth Army up the Italian peninsula, for example, were typically located between twenty and fifty-five kilometers from the battle area.[3]

There is even less logic in circumscribing the use of women in units operating in the corps area (normally over fifty-five kilometers from the front line). Moreover, current limitation of women's activities on physical grounds is highly arbitrary and, until physical standards are better defined, unduly restrictive.

The effects of modifying these limitations can be quantified.

ONE SUGGESTED MODIFICATION. By opening *noncombat* jobs in units expected to operate *outside* the brigade area, women would have access to an additional 81,000 billets, or a total of 136,000. Reducing the requirements for additional billets currently reserved for men (for management reasons and for the "pipeline") would release a further 39,000 positions. Hence, at least 175,000 Army jobs (one-fourth of all enlisted jobs and over one-third of all enlisted noncombatant positions) could be filled by women—more than a threefold increase in the goal set by the Army, as summarized in table 8-2.

A FURTHER MODIFICATION. Going one step further, if restrictions on the use of women were limited to combat specialties only, and their assignment to *noncombat* specialties in *all* units—including those in the brigade

---

1. Department of the Army, *Army Regulation 600-200,* Change 44, July 1, 1971, p. 3-10.
2. Ibid., Change 52, December 16, 1974.
3. Mattie Treadwell, *The Women's Army Corps* (Department of the Army, Office of the Chief of Military History, 1954), p. 367.

**Table 8-2. Projected Number of Army Enlisted Jobs Open to Women,
Current Estimate and Modified Proposal**

Thousands

Type of enlisted jobs	Positions available to women	
	Current estimate	Modified proposal
Total (including pipeline)	**676**	**676**
Less jobs closed to women	415	334
All jobs in combat units	261	261
Combat jobs in noncombat units	20	20
Geographical guidelines	68	. . .
Pipeline allowance	66	53
Less jobs reserved for men	206	167
Rotation base requirements	23	18
Career development	150	121
Pipeline allowance	33	28
Total number enlisted jobs open to women	**55**	**175**

Sources: Current estimates, chapter 3; modified proposal, see text. The assumption is made that positions reserved for rotation base and career development would decrease proportionately to the decrease in the number of billets closed to women and that pipeline positions would decrease proportionately to the decrease in total billets in each category.

area—were considered appropriate, another 110,000 jobs would be opened to women. That would mean that up to 50 percent of all enlisted positions could conceivably be filled by women without disrupting male assignment and career development patterns.

Women in the Navy

In the case of the Navy, job opportunities for women are limited because they cannot serve at sea. Of 152,000 shore billets identified, women, according to the Navy, can only occupy about 21,000, lest men's sea-shore rotation and career development patterns be disturbed.

The Navy's calculation is based on a set of assumptions, at least two of which appear to be more conservative than is necessary. First, the number of shore billets to be reserved for men depends largely on the frequency with which men are rotated between sea and shore duty. The current Navy calculation is based on an assignment pattern of thirty-six months at sea followed by thirty-six months ashore—a goal established during the Zumwalt era. Although sailors in some skills have been able to maintain that pattern of rotation, naval personnel in general have traditionally spent more time at sea than on shore, and by current experience spend on average about forty-eight months at sea for every thirty months ashore.

Second, to avoid clustering a disproportionate number of women in the upper grades in the future, the number entering the lower grades is currently limited. Obviously, this calculation depends on the proportion of women who remain in the Navy long enough to attain the higher grades. Current Navy methodology embodies the assumption that 50 percent of the enlisted women who enter the Navy will complete their first term of service and reenlist—a retention rate that far exceeds recent experience.

ONE SUGGESTED MODIFICATION. By adopting two more realistic assumptions—say, a rotation of forty-eight months at sea and thirty-six months on shore and a 25 percent retention rate—the number of billets that could be occupied by either men or women under existing policies could well be doubled. This would make available at least another 20,000 positions to women. Moreover, to keep say, 40,000 women on the job, the Navy would need an additional 2,500 to offset those women who would be expected to be in a travel or patient status at any point in time.

A FURTHER MODIFICATION. To go much beyond 42,500, however, would mean that current sea-duty restrictions would have to be modified. If the statutory restriction excluding women from all naval vessels were altered to exclude only "combat" vessels, more billets would be sex-neutral. For example, women could fill another 40,000 billets if duty aboard support ships—underway replenishment and auxiliary vessels— were made available to them and sea-duty, "male-only" billets reduced from 230,000 to about 190,000.[4]

Reducing the number of jobs restricted to men would also reduce by 20,000 the number reserved for men for rotation and management reasons. Thus an estimated total of 100,000 billets—five times the current goal—could be opened to women.

Women in the Marine Corps

Under today's practices, the Marine Corps, of all the military services, is least capable of using women. It is inhibited by implicit limitations governing the deployment of women in both the Army and the Navy: women

4. Based on data appearing in *Fiscal Year 1977 Authorization for Military Procurement, Research and Development, and Active Duty, Selected Reserve and Civilian Personnel Strengths,* Hearings before the Senate Committee on Armed Services, 94:2, pt. 7 (GPO, 1976), p. 4019.

Table 8-3. Enlisted Women in the Armed Forces, Announced Goals and Estimated Potential Utilization

Service	Announced goals for women's participation		Estimated potential utilization of women	
	Number (thousands)	Percent of total strength	Number (thousands)	Percent of total strength
Army	50.4	7.4	175.0	25.9
Navy	21.1	4.5	42.5	9.2
Marine Corps	6.7	3.9	15.0	8.8
Air Force	48.2	10.1	363.0	76.1
Total	126.4	7.1	595.5	33.3

Sources: Announced goals, OASD, Manpower and Reserve Affairs, "Use of Women in the Military"; estimated goals, see text.

cannot serve on board ship nor do they operate near the front line. Furthermore, the Corps has relatively few noncombat billets available since it depends on the Navy for much of its support. Nonetheless, there are some 30,000 enlisted jobs in base operations, command, and logistics units; perhaps half could be filled by women. If, as in the case of the Army, noncombat billets in combat units were available then the potential number of women in the Corps would be even larger.

Women in the Air Force

Finally, the Air Force, confronted with few restrictions on the sex composition of its enlisted component, could accommodate a far greater proportion of women than the other services. As indicated in chapter 3, women could vie for 363,000 enlisted jobs without violating current Air Force policies. And once overseas housing problems are alleviated, close to 450,000, or 94 percent of all Air Force enlisted jobs, could be opened to women.

Maximum Potential Utilization under Current Policies

Quotas for women currently operating for each of the services fall far short of potential utilization under more appropriate policy guidelines. Without radically departing from current policies and practices, and without disrupting the rotation and career opportunities for men, it is estimated that close to 600,000 military enlisted jobs, compared with the planned 126,400, could *potentially* be filled by women, as shown in table 8-3.

Of these jobs, the number that women could be expected to fill would depend on the relative qualifications of prospective volunteers. Hence, it is important that steps be taken by the Pentagon to ensure that women are made aware of the available opportunities and that they are encouraged to enter these specialties. Furthermore, realistic sex-neutral physical and operational standards have to be developed and better measures devised for predicting the ability of people to meet stated requirements.

Even if only half of the interchangeable positions were to be occupied by women, the total number of enlisted women in the military services would more than double the current quotas. And it is conceivable that the number of military enlisted women could eventually reach 400,000, or 22 percent of the force.[5] Beyond this range, however, further expansion would depend on a resolution of the combat issue.

Women as Warriors? Narrowing the Uncertainties

The sex composition of the armed forces is shaped, in the last analysis, by the prohibitions on the assignment of women to so-called combat occupations or to units whose main function is loosely related to combat. Whether these blanket sex distinctions are appropriate in today's rapidly changing society needs investigation.

The question is extremely complex, involving a cross-cut of social and military factors. Two powerful social forces are in collision: the push for women's equal rights is in conflict with deeply rooted traditions that question the propriety of women under arms. That the body politic supports equal opportunity *in principle* is indisputable; virtually every public opinion poll taken on the subject confirms it. However, the extent to which people will accept equality *in practice,* including committing women to combat, is less clear; virtually no public opinion polls have been taken on the subject. And despite two opportunities to interpret and clarify the "national will"—during the debates on the Equal Rights Amendment and

5. Obviously, these are long-term prospects. An expansion of the number of women in the military would have to be accomplished gradually to avoid clustering large numbers of women at the same grade and with the same experience level. The appropriate rate of increase would depend on many management factors, which would vary among the services. On balance, it seems reasonable to expect that the number of military women could be expanded at a rate that would double their present number within three to five years and reach 400,000—if that goal is deemed appropriate—within ten years.

the proposal to admit women to attend the nation's military academies—the question remains unresolved.

Also at odds are two more practical issues related to national security: the budgetary advantages of recruiting more women are at variance with perceived risks to the U.S. national interest. Were women to constitute a larger proportion of the military establishment, it is clear that personnel quality (measured by educational level and general intelligence and aptitude) would improve. Less certain, however, are the overall implications for military effectiveness. Little is known about how women will perform combat tasks, and even less about how they will affect combat unit performance.

These issues will not be easy to resolve. Many of the controversies elude theoretical solution; experience will have to provide the answers. It is clearly up to Congress to take the initiative since the military services seem reluctant to do so themselves.

An Experimental Program

A reasonable first step might be for the Department of Defense to set up an experimental program for each military service, which would be required to integrate selected combat units that currently exclude women. The test should be designed to find out, first, how many women would volunteer for the positions available in these units and, second, what effect they would have on unit performance.

UNDERLYING PRINCIPLES. The exact specifications of the program would have to be worked out between Congress and the Pentagon, but certain broad principles should govern the experiment. The test should be limited, on the one hand, to ensure that combat effectiveness is not unduly diminished but it should be sufficiently extensive, on the other, to provide a valid sample. The Army and Marine Corps each might integrate several maneuver battalions, the Navy might integrate ship's companies on several vessels, and the Air Force might integrate ballistic missile launch crews and aircrews in, say, a fighter and bomber squadron.

There is little precedent for such an experiment so that the design would have to be carefully considered. Criteria for selection, classification, and assignment of personnel, both men and women, would be important as would the measures of effectiveness to be used. Particular attention ought to be paid to the proportions of men and women in the units. The military services would have to redirect current recruiting practices to publicize these openings to civilian women; one important facet of the test would be to find out how many women are willing to serve in such combat or seagoing units. Military planners would have to develop realistic physical and operational standards to determine the requirements for effective performance, and also the methods to measure people's ability to meet such standards. Finally, the criteria for assessing the comparative effectiveness of integrated and nonintegrated units would have to be established.

POSSIBLE PROBLEMS. The difficulties involved in assessing individual and organizational effectiveness are apparent from the findings of this study. Thus, despite the possibility for exploiting state-of-the-art improvements in industrial engineering and in the behavioral sciences, comparative analyses of effectiveness should not be expected to pass tests of scientific rigor. The relative proficiency of the units could be evaluated using criteria similar to those now employed to scale the effectiveness of all-male units.[6] Obviously, all measurements would be made under peacetime conditions; there would be no measure of women's ability to withstand the degrees of stress inherent in each category of combat. However, to date, predicting men's performance under combat conditions gives rise to uncertainties of its own.

The program would probably take several years to complete. It would take time to recruit and train women in the necessary skills; at the extreme, for example, about two years are needed to train a fighter pilot. Initially, of course, women would be working mainly at the apprentice and journeyman skill levels and at the lower grades. This situation, which caused problems during the *Sanctuary* experiment discussed in chapter 7, would persist until women had attained enough experience to become supervisors.

During the test, particular attention should be given to the relationship between pregnancy and performance. Current policies that permit pregnant women to remain on the job for a good part of their prenatal period may have to be reassessed. These policies were formulated at a time when women were assigned mainly to sedentary and light duties; whether these policies are appropriate for women assigned to combat units is a separate question to be evaluated.

---

6. All of the services now evaluate their combat units based on measures of merit incorporating such things as scorable competitive exercises, accuracy of weapons delivery systems, frequency of equipment failure, and effectiveness of the supply system.

Legislative Changes

The experiment described above would require that current statutes be modified. Appropriate sections might be changed quite simply to permit exceptions to current provisions. Alternatively, it could be argued that these restrictions should be eliminated entirely. There is no reason to bar the use of women aboard naval vessels or as members of combat aircrews inasmuch as similar legislative constraints are not imposed upon ground combat forces. It would seem only logical that the secretaries of the Navy and Air Force be allowed the same latitude in using their personnel resources as that currently allowed the secretary of the Army.

Moreover, it can be argued that the restrictions are superfluous in any event. As has been demonstrated, even though the restrictions have not been codified, the Army is not clamoring to move women into combat roles. Indeed, it is safe to conclude that combat jobs would be opened to women only under external pressures.

The direction for the test program should be provided for in separate legislation. Although this could be achieved through an amendment to some related legislation, it would be more appropriate for a matter of such importance that the programs be referred to the respective armed services committees as a separate bill for full deliberation. Formal hearings should be held, with participation by military witnesses, public interest groups, and informed experts.

ULTIMATELY, CONGRESS is in the best position to address the questions posed in this study, to evaluate the social and national security trade-offs, and to prescribe a program for moving toward an optimum utilization of women in the U.S. military establishment.

Congress has a twofold responsibility. If it fails to meet its obligations then, first, American women will continue to be denied equal opportunities for social and financial betterment; and, second, future defense budgets may be larger than necessary, the size of the U.S. armed forces may have to be reduced, or the nation may be forced to return to conscription.

Foreign Experience:
A Synopsis

Below are brief descriptions of women's roles in the military in twenty-five countries. Unless otherwise indicated, the material presented relies on information received in response to a 1976 questionnaire circulated to foreign embassies in Washington, D.C., supplemented by unclassified information on Eastern European nations from the U.S. Defense Intelligence Agency. The sole purpose here is to provide readers with a synopsis of foreign experience as a basis of comparison with the situation in the United States.

Many countries, especially those belonging to the Warsaw Pact, do not divulge data on their military establishments, and outside estimates are often conflicting. Such disparities are necessarily reflected in the data.

The information submitted has been divided, where applicable, into descriptions of (a) women's current participation in the military, and (b) their participation in time of conflict, generally in World War II. Table A-1 tabulates the data available in 1976.

The North Atlantic Treaty Organization

The North Atlantic Treaty signed in 1949 by Belgium, Canada, Denmark, France, Iceland, Italy, Luxembourg, the Netherlands, Norway, Portugal, the United Kingdom, and the United States unites Western Europe and North America in a protective security agreement against threats and armed attack. Greece and Turkey joined NATO in 1952 and West Germany in 1955. In 1976, NATO countries, except Iceland, Italy, Luxembourg, and Portugal, had women in the armed forces.

At the 1975 NATO Conference of Senior Service Women, expectations were raised that more women would be used in the NATO armed

Table A-1. Women in the Military, Selected Countries, 1976[a]

Country	Military strength[b]		Women as a percentage of total strength
	Total	Women	
Australia	69,350	3,500	5.0
Belgium	88,300	600	d
Canada	77,900	3,450	4.4
China, Republic of (Taiwan)	470,000	12,500	2.7
Denmark	34,700	550	1.6
France	512,900	8,550	1.7
Germany, Federal Republic of	495,000	c	d
Greece	199,500	0	0
Israel	158,500	8,000	5.0
Italy	352,000	0	0
Japan	235,000	2,300	1.0
Netherlands	112,200	1,900	1.7
New Zealand	12,600	750	5.8
Norway	39,000	1,250	3.2
Philippines	78,000	450	d
Portugal	59,800	0	0
Soviet Union	4,410,000	10,000	d
Turkey	480,000	100	d
United Kingdom	344,150	14,700	4.3
United States	2,086,700	108,800	5.2
Yugoslavia	250,000	2,600	1.0

Sources: Total military strength, except Soviet Union, International Institute for Strategic Studies, *The Military Balance 1976–1977* (London: IISS, 1976); Soviet Union, David Smith, "Soviet Military Manpower," *Air Force*, vol. 60 (March 1977), p. 78. Figures on women's participation based largely on authors' correspondence with appropriate embassies in Washington, D.C.; supplementary data in *The Military Balance 1976–1977;* Verna J. Dickerson, "The Role of Women in the Defense Force of Israel" (U.S. Army War College, May 1974; processed); and U.S. Defense Intelligence Agency, "Women in the Soviet Armed Forces," DDI-1100-109-76 (DIA, March 1976; processed), p. 5.

a. Includes only those nations for which data on women are available.

b. Rounded to nearest fifty people; includes active strength only; reserves, paramilitary forces, and the like are excluded.

c. Less than fifty.

d. Less than 1 percent.

forces. The data appear to corroborate this. In 1973, for example, seven countries had no women in the military whereas by 1975 there were only four. These are modest gains. No NATO country today employs military women as combatants nor is such a move envisaged. In fact, senior military women attending a 1973 conference in Brussels supported a no-combat role except in emergencies. On the other hand, they did support an expanded employment policy for NATO military women.[1] And the addition of military women to the forces in Belgium, the Federal Republic

1. *NATO Conference of Senior Service Women Officers of the Alliance* (Copenhagen, Hørsholm Bogtrykkeri for the Danish Women's Air Force, 1974), pp. 74–75; ibid. (London: United Kingdom Women's Services, 1976).

of Germany (as nurses), Greece (as nurses), and to the Netherlands' current naval test program indicates some expansion.

Belgium

CURRENT PARTICIPATION. The Belgian government first recruited women in 1974. As in the United States, its rationale was based on military need and egalitarian considerations. By 1975, 605 women had been recruited (less than 1 percent of 88,300 personnel in the armed forces), with plans to add 1,000 women a year until a total of 5,000, or approximately 5 percent of the total force level, is reached. Women are excluded from combat, and there are laws governing their use in heavy or dangerous work, maternity provisions, and regulations to protect them in war as noncombatants. Women can be assigned to noncombat jobs in the air force, navy, or army; their training is the same as that for men except for weapons training, which is solely for national defense. In 1976, there were no plans to recruit women officers, the highest rank attainable was that of corporal.

Canada

CURRENT PARTICIPATION. In 1966 the Canadian forces combined to form the unified Canadian Armed Force composed of personnel who volunteer for sea, land, or air duties. In 1976 women constituted over 4 percent of this military force of 77,900. There were also more than 4,300 women in the reserve forces. Their primary purpose was to serve as a labor pool of individuals with special skills and abilities, rather than releasing men to fight.

The trend in Canada is to make greater use of its women in the military. The goals for 1984 are to raise the proportion of women to around 10 percent of force strength and to open up more job opportunities. In February 1976, eighteen of the twenty-seven occupations for officers and sixty-two of ninety-eight trades for enlisted personnel were made available to women.

Terms of service are the same, with wages based on equal pay for equal responsibilities. A Canadian officer can advance through the ranks without the dual combat-staff jobs required in the United States. The emphasis is on specialization and officers, including women, can advance to top positions without actually fighting or participating in combat.

Attempts are being made to integrate male and female training including defensive weapons training and some field fighting. While women officers do not attend military colleges, subsidized university training is available at civilian colleges. Women officers and senior noncommissioned officers attend military staff courses and leadership schools on an integrated basis.

Until 1971 only single women could enlist but a new policy permits married women, even those with children, to do so. Maternity benefits provide up to fifteen weeks' leave without pay, during which full medical coverage and unemployment benefits are available. Upon return to duty rigid rules require unrestricted service regardless of family responsibilities. Those women unable to comply with these rules are released from service.

PARTICIPATION IN TIME OF CONFLICT. In World War II the professed purpose was to release men for combat duties. While women's scope of employment was limited at the outset, it included even technical jobs as the war progressed. Of the eighty trades in the air force, sixty-six were open to women; army women served in antiaircraft units, coast artillery regiments, and signal units. Women were even employed in rear areas of theaters of war such as in Italy and Northwest Europe. They also served in the United States and Britain. By 1944 there were 33,000 women in uniform: 6,000 in the navy, 12,000 in the army, and 15,000 in the air force. After demobilization in 1946, women were not again recruited until 1951 when Canada made its commitment to NATO and the United Nations in Korea. By 1955, 5,490 women were in service, the majority working in administration, medical services, and logistics.

Denmark

CURRENT PARTICIPATION. In 1976 women constituted about 1.7 percent of the 34,700 personnel in the defense force. They can either enroll in the three civilian women's services of the home guard or, since 1969, enlist as regulars in the armed services. Some are employed full time whereas others are in the reserve. In case of war all members of the women's services will serve as military personnel with the same obligations and rights as males. About 16 percent of the 67,752 in the home guard are women.

Women's training is the joint responsibility of the home guard, the armed services, and the women's services under the director of the women's army corps. They are only trained to use arms in times of emergency, not as combatants.

The qualifications for enlistment are the same for men and women. They have to be Danish citizens, between eighteen and twenty-six years of age, in good health, and have had nine years of schooling. Officers must have four months of basic training, six months at sergeant school, serve as sergeant for six months, and then complete officers' school. Women can also attend the Danish military academy.

Military women are restricted to assignments in the army at brigade level or higher, and they cannot serve aboard ships or in aircraft. However, military regulars (men and women) are reportedly trained in self-defense, shooting, and biological warfare, and they are armed with submachine guns. The participation of women as regular military members of the Danish armed forces is expected to expand with the new defense acts projected for sometime in 1977.

France

CURRENT PARTICIPATION. Women are accorded the same rights and, in principle, have the same obligations as men; but only men have to undergo military training. However, a 1971 law established a national military service for women which allows women to *volunteer* for a one-year military commitment in the regular French army similar to that *required* of men. By 1976 there had been only a few volunteers for the army, about thirty for the navy, and around six hundred for the air force.

Another women's organization, the women's military corps (Personnels féminines des Armées) is an outgrowth of the fusion in 1944 of the French women's army corps, the French corps of volunteers in London, and the French resistance; it became affiliated with the French army in 1972 when women were accorded essentially the same military status as men except that, by decree in 1973, they were restricted in rank and assignment (no sea or combat duty), and different selection and age criteria were set. The corps constitutes less than 2 percent of the 513,000 in the French defense forces. Jobs now open to women range from telecommunications specialist, data processor, and air controller to the significant number still in administration and personnel.

PARTICIPATION IN TIME OF CONFLICT. French women participated in World War II as early as 1939 when civilian women served with the army mainly as drivers, medical personnel, and social workers, even in the war zones. The women considered themselves as members of the women's armed forces although they had no military status. But, in 1940, with the great manpower shortage, women were permitted to volunteer as auxiliaries in certain areas: general staff, artillery, engineering, and health service for a period of one year or for the duration of hostilities. Later, in London in 1940 the French liberation forces were established, and women were given the chance to join the French corps of volunteers as part of the army. They were trained by the British Auxiliary Territorial Service in nearly all categories of employment, and some saw duty in Algeria and Tunisia.

French women also served in Italy and in the resistance movement. Finally, after the liberation of France, a 1944 act gave the women's various services legitimate status. After World War II, women saw duty in Algeria and in the Indochinese war. In the latter, some served as liaison pilots.

Federal Republic of Germany

CURRENT PARTICIPATION. In 1975 the Federal Republic of Germany (FRG) appointed twenty-two female medical officers. These women (fourteen in the army, three in the navy, five in the air force) are the only females in West Germany's armed forces numbering 495,000. No greater participation is anticipated.

PARTICIPATION IN TIME OF CONFLICT. Women were conscripted both for the military services and the industrial labor market during World War II. Although German women served with the armed forces as civilians who were not subject to all military regulations, their organization resembled that of women's military auxiliary forces in other countries.

Many women served as noncombatants assigned to the replacement rather than the field army subject to National Service regulations. Their jobs ranged from rolling bandages to packing gunpowder. Another group, unmarried women between seventeen and twenty-five years of age, were employed as armed forces auxiliaries. Generally, they were assigned in closed groups of fifty or more and supervised by the Reich Labor Force. Not only was their work different (such as servicing and operating searchlight and antiaircraft batteries), but they also received pocket money, clothing allowance, and uniforms.

Each Wehrmacht established its own women's auxiliary which served all over Germany and in occupied territories. They were considered members, although noncombatants, of the armed forces. There was no differentiation in the employment of married and unmarried women except that married women did not have to serve in occupied territory. Pregnant women could remain in occupied territories until their fifth month of pregnancy whereupon they returned home and worked for the war effort as civilians.

It is difficult to estimate the number of women who served militarily, but, since women in the Reich Labor Force and National Service assigned to the Wehrmacht performed functions assigned to military women of other countries, one can speculate that the 150,000 women in the National Service and the 100,000 in the Reich Labor Force and other volunteer auxiliaries constituted about 3 percent of the 9.6 million individuals in the German armed forces of World War II. Reports do point out, however, that even though women were conscripted for work in industry and auxiliaries to the armed forces, they were used to "release a man to fight" and not as part of a planned national policy.[2]

Greece

CURRENT PARTICIPATION. Greece has no women serving with the Hellenic Armed Forces Command except the nurse corps. Established in 1946, the corps worked exclusively with the Army until 1956 when a policy change authorized their assignment to navy and air force units. In 1971 the corps was unified under one directorate headed by a female lieutenant colonel.

PARTICIPATION IN TIME OF CONFLICT. Nurses served in World War II as civilian workers with the military hospitals and as volunteers at military posts. They had no military status, however, until after the war.

Netherlands

CURRENT PARTICIPATION. The Netherlands have regular, fully integrated services in the army (MILVA), navy (MARVA), and air force (LUBA), except for separately executed basic training and combat re-

2. For a more complete account, see: Ursula von Gersdorff, *Frauen im Kriegsdienst, 1914–1945* (Stuttgart: Deutsche Verlags-Anstalt, 1969); Hierl Konstantin, *Idea and Formation of Labor Service* (Germany: U.S. Army, Historical Division, 1946); August Schalkaeuser, *German Women in War Service during World War II* (Germany: U.S. Army, Historical Division, 1949).

strictions. However, the MARVA is currently considering a test program to use women in noncombat jobs on supply ships. If such a test is successful the expansion of women's role in MARVA appears likely. Women, in 1976, constituted approximately 1.7 percent of the Netherlands' defense force of 112,200. They could be assigned to the various NATO headquarters, as well as to the staffs of the various Netherlands attachés. They work in communications, administration, medicine, meteorology, and electronics. The previous practice of using enlisted women as stewards, cooks, and the like has been discontinued. Women do not attend the military academies.

PARTICIPATION IN TIME OF CONFLICT. During World War II women served with the Netherlands military services as volunteers, and their method of organization was based on Australian experience. However, in 1944, the women's section of MARVA was established in London modeled after the British Women's Royal Naval Service. All training centers were moved to the Netherlands in 1946. From 1945 to 1949 some of these women were deployed to the former Netherlands East Indies.

Norway

CURRENT PARTICIPATION. Norway is one of the few countries to poll its citizens concerning women in the military. A 1975 Gallup poll indicated that 70 percent of the Norwegians want women in the armed forces and 53 percent consider that they should be conscripted. A 1957 decree had permitted women to take jobs as civilians in the armed forces in peacetime. Those desiring wartime service could make contracts for wartime mobilization and were thereby accorded military status. However, in 1976 the Norwegian Parliament approved a bill that allows women to serve directly in the armed services. Its main purpose is to ensure that women are protected under international convention. In 1976 about 3 percent of Norway's armed forces of 39,000 were women.

Women serve in the armed forces in four categories: in the KIF (women in the armed forces) military, the KIF reserve, the KIF for the home guard, and as civilian employees. Except that they are volunteers and restricted to noncombat duties, the KIF military are fully integrated with the men's units. KIF reserves consist of civilian women in the armed forces under contract to serve as military personnel in time of war, women who want to train for military wartime service, and former servicewomen. Civilian women employed by the military who wish to retain their civilian status even in wartime are known as "lotter" and organized through the Norwegian women's voluntary service in local communities. The home guard administers their service for military defense.

The 1976 legislation provides for equal pay and rank with men, as well as special provisions for women during pregnancy and equal competition for jobs. But women cannot take any combat-related jobs, nor is allowance made for their promotion. Training and education are coeducational except for basic military training and combat courses. Women who want the same basic training as the men may volunteer for it but, as in many other countries, weapons training is for defense only. Projected levels for women's participation in peacetime are approximately 3,500 officers and noncommissioned officers and 12,000 other ranks.

Turkey

CURRENT PARTICIPATION. There are only about one hundred female officers in the Turkish armed forces whose assignments are limited to signal, supply, ordnance, welfare, and medical services at the headquarters level. They share a similar status to their male counterparts.

In past years women could serve in less traditional areas; reportedly at one time they were trained as combat pilots.

United Kingdom

CURRENT PARTICIPATION. The "no combat" role prevalent throughout the history of women's participation in the military still prevailed in 1976, despite the impetus provided by the women's movement. The latter led, however, to the integration of all-women's units into the regular army. The Royal Navy, on the other hand, still retains the independent Women's Royal Naval Service that is trained and administered by a woman director. The Women's Royal Air Force has always been an integral part of the RAF. In 1976 women constituted only slightly over 4 percent of Britain's military establishment, 344,150 strong. A recent defense review of the U.K. armed forces indicates no plans for expansion in the near future, either male or female.

Most jobs for women follow the traditional pattern, but the Navy has included some women in such nontraditional areas as tactical training for women officers and weapons system analysis for all women. The air force has one aircrew job, that of loadmaster, open to women. In 1976–77 the

British army had over two hundred women in the Ulster Defense Regiment, operating in Northern Ireland. Their duties generally involved communications, border patrols, and operating at vehicle checkpoints. This is the first time that women have been directly recruited for a British regiment rather than being assigned from the Women's Royal Army Corps. For the most part they were accorded equal treatment with the men except that they did not carry weapons. This use of women in an essentially combat environment has been considered successful and may have implications for the future continuation of separate structures for women's services.

In 1975 women theoretically gained equal basic pay with their male counterparts. This came as part of a general pay review that equalized military pay for married and single individuals and offered a salary scale equivalent to civilian employment. However, an additional element of basic pay termed the "X" factor is designed to compensate for the rigors of military life—exposure to danger, turbulence, and restrictions on personal freedom. Women receive a 5 percent "X" factor and men receive 10 percent.

Also under review (because of recent developments in the United States and Canada) are policies governing marriage, children, and continuing a career in the military.

PARTICIPATION IN TIME OF CONFLICT. The United Kingdom was one of four countries (the others are Germany, the USSR, and later Israel) that reluctantly developed a national policy to conscript women during wartime, either for the military or for civilian work. Between 1941 and 1945, approximately 125,000 women were inducted into military service and another 430,000 volunteered. Thus women constituted about 12 percent of the 4.6 million military personnel strength.

Women in the Auxiliary Territorial Service, the Women's Royal Navy Service, and the Women's Auxiliary Air Force first served as drivers, cooks, orderlies, and telephone operators. Later, as the manpower shortage became greater, they worked in ordnance maintenance and repair, and as bricklayers, electrical engineers, and range finders and fire controllers in antiaircraft batteries. Some women volunteers serving in integrated antiaircraft artillery batteries saw action both at home and overseas, suffered casualties, or became prisoners of war. However, despite their close proximity to actual combat, women were never considered to be in a direct combat role.

The Warsaw Pact Countries

The Warsaw Pact was signed in 1955 by the Soviet Union, Albania, Bulgaria, Czechoslovakia, East Germany, Hungary, Poland, and Romania as a multilateral military alliance pledged to the defense of the European territories of its member states. Albania left the Warsaw Pact in 1968.

Assessing the role of women in Warsaw Pact countries poses difficulties because of the dearth of information, and because these countries utilize a total defense program that includes a wide spectrum of civilian organizations dedicated to some phase of training for national defense in which many women participate. The complex interrelationship between these civilian national defense organizations and the regular military services makes it even more difficult to compare the role of women in the Warsaw Pact and NATO countries. Available data indicates a very limited role for women in the military services both in numbers and types of occupations. They are believed to perform auxiliary roles in the traditional "female" occupations.

Union of Soviet Socialist Republics

CURRENT PARTICIPATION. Under the USSR constitution Soviet women are theoretically guaranteed equal rights with men in all spheres of life. In practice, however, they are relegated to the more traditional roles. Today's Soviet military women resemble their counterparts in other countries—they are an adjunct labor resource to supplement the male force, and there are fewer of them proportionately than in many Western countries. Available evidence indicates that the 1976 active-duty female military strength was approximately 10,000.

All women between the ages of nineteen and forty years of age with medical, veterinary, and special training have to register and are subject to induction into the military reserve. They are obligated to undergo periodic training and are subject to recall in time of war. No published information is apparently available on the actual types of skills that make women subject to induction or on the numbers in the reserves. However, it is known that, in 1973, about 74 percent had either a special skill or higher education, that 40 percent of all scientific workers were women, and that there were 559,000 female doctors.[3] It is reasonable to assume from these figures therefore that a significant number of Soviet women were trained in the reserves.

Soviet women who enlist must be physically fit and between the ages of nineteen and twenty-five; they must have had at least a seventh-grade education. They cannot attend officer schools. The initial two-year enlistment term can be extended an additional two years with automatic enrollment in the reserves until the age of forty.

Regulations, allowances, and promotions *appear* to be the same for both sexes, but women's assignments and their numbers are restricted compared with those of men—and the positions, of course, determine pay.

Women are trained in the more traditional specialties, primarily for medical, administrative, communications, and other support jobs. They take part in training drills, field trips, and attend all-women classes in political, combat, and physical training. But they are prohibited from serving aboard combat ships and planes and cannot continue on active duty either during or after pregnancy, at which time they are released to reserve units.

PARTICIPATION IN TIME OF CONFLICT. In the Soviet Union, as elsewhere, men and women were no longer segregated in wartime by type of employment. Women were conscripted in World War II and used extensively not only in agriculture and industry but even at the front line. There was the common progression from the more traditional assignments at the beginning of the war to actual combat duty in both mixed and all-female units as the pressure of conflict increased the need for manpower. By 1945 women constituted 51 percent of the industrial labor force, working in practically every industry. Their peak strength in the military reached the million mark out of a total force strength of twelve million.

Over 800,000 women served in the Red Army as tank crewmembers, machine gunners, snipers, and members of artillery crews, as well as in the more conventional pursuits. Many served in air defense units, they formed from 60 to 80 percent of the Communist youth organization (Komosol), carrying weapons and often coming under fire. They were also used as scouts and snipers with the partisan forces and even did demolition work. These women were trained either in schools set up by the Komosol to teach women to fight side by side with the regular forces, or by civilian organizations. The Red Cross, for example, trained hun-

3. "Women in the USSR," *Soviet Military Review* (March 1976), p. 46.

dreds of thousands of nurses and medical assistants; sports clubs trained 600,000 women in physical culture; more than 150 air clubs (of which every fourth member was a woman) trained women pilots and mechanics.

Among the women in the air force were accredited pilots who were formed into three all-female regiments: a fighter regiment, a short-range day bomber unit, and a night light-bomber unit. They all saw action. The 586th Women's Air Fighter Regiment, for instance, was stationed first on the banks of the Volga River and later near Vienna. The regiment accompanied Soviet combat units and provided air cover for a number of Soviet and East European cities, as well as important river crossings.[4]

Bulgaria

CURRENT PARTICIPATION. A 1958 law provides for the conscription of women. Whether it is in effect cannot be verified; the presence of Major General Polina Nedyalkova, one of the most famous Soviet tank commanders during World War II, would indicate that there was some participation. She returned to her native Bulgaria in 1952.

Theoretically, women are called up to fill specialties when shortages occur, and those between nineteen and forty-five, accepted for limited active duty, are assigned to the reserve upon completion of their tour of service.

The reserves are categorized as (1) those men who have completed military service or who have specialized training skills, and (2) male draftees not yet in service, noncombatants (those accepted for noncombat duty in wartime), and women (aged nineteen to forty-five years) who have served in the military.

Czechoslovakia

CURRENT PARTICIPATION. Women between the ages of eighteen and twenty with a secondary general education may enlist. They must pass an

4. Information on Soviet women during World War II is from "Soviet Women in the Great Patriotic War," *Soviet Military Review* (March 1975), pp. 42–45; "Soviet Women at War," *Anglo-Soviet Journal,* vol. 3 (April–June 1942), pp. 71–82; "Heroines of an Air Regiment," in *Antiaircraft Defense Herald* (March 1972), pp. 145–47; U.S. Defense Intelligence Agency, "Women in the Soviet Armed Forces," DDI-1100-109-76 (DIA, March 1976; processed); Alexi Flerovsky, "Women Flyers of Fighter Planes," *Soviet Life* (May 1975), pp. 28–29; V. Mitroshenkov, "They were First," *Soviet Military Review* (March 1969), p. 22; E. Meos, "Russian Women Fighter Pilots," *Flight International* (December 27, 1962), pp. 1019–20.

entrance exam that includes physical tests of endurance. The Czecho-slovakian army does not have a special women's army corps; women are assigned to those units involving their specialties.

Women receive twelve months' training, half of which is theoretical and half of which is specialized practical. During this period they have the same status as basic service soldiers, have room (dormitory style), board, and clothing. Upon completion of training they incur a three-year obligation as "noncommissioned officers in further service" rather than as career officers.

Women can be trained as air dispatchers, plotters, radio operators, signalers, and administrative workers. There are no data on the actual number of women employed in 1976; the latest information is that, after a military campaign drive in 1966, there were reportedly 300 percent more applicants than there were jobs available. Women can apparently revert to reserve status after three years or continue their military careers; in some instances (as in 1966) some specialty shortages have led to an active commitment for as long as ten years.

German Democratic Republic

CURRENT PARTICIPATION. Since the establishment of East Germany's army, known as the National People's Army (NVA), in 1956, women have presumably served in its ranks. In 1962 a defense obligation law required the conscription of women between the ages of eighteen and fifty in an emergency. During normal periods, women may volunteer as extended-term (three-year minimum) soldiers or as career (ten-year minimum) soldiers. Officers may serve up to twenty-five years although a three-, six- or ten-year period is an available option. The extent of women's participation in the army is estimated at about 560 women.

Pay and allowances for both men and women are based on grade, position, and length of service. The highest rank an enlisted woman can attain is that of staff sergeant, if on extended duty, and that of master sergeant, if a careerist. Officers on limited duty may expect to reach captain with a few careerists attaining higher rank.

Women are not eligible to attend the military academy in Dresden. Basic training depends upon the specialty, and in some specialties those with prior civilian experience are given preference. In addition to basic training, women receive routine training once a week that includes political training, first aid, firing exercises, sports, weapons and defensive combat training.

Enlisted women are usually found in traditional occupations on the staff of service branches, military districts, subdistricts, area commands, and with border organizations. The three major areas in which the women serve are administration (as clerks, stenographers, secretaries), communications (as telephone and radio operators, teletypists, and in the mail and carrier service), and medical services (as nurses, medical, dental, and veterinary assistants, and in other hospital jobs). A few work in intelligence, especially in imagery interpretation, and a few women officers are serving as physicians and interpreters.

PARTICIPATION IN TIME OF CONFLICT. See Federal Republic of Germany for a description of experience in World War II.

Hungary

CURRENT PARTICIPATION. Reports in 1976 indicated that a bill had been introduced requiring all citizens to register in peacetime as well as during emergencies. Women with special skills, such as those in health care and telecommunications, were to be subject to call-up until they reached the age of forty-five. They could, however, volunteer for a two-year term of service and then return to the reserves. Reservists might be called up once every three years for further training, and at any time for short exercises.

In addition, the law would provide for national defense instruction for young people (presumably including women) who had not yet done their military service.

Romania

CURRENT PARTICIPATION. Women can join the Romanian Army as career officers and noncommissioned officers under the 1972 law organizing national defense. Women are also subject to conscription and all those attending college-level institutes, while exempt, are subject to military training during their school years. After nine months' military conscription they are then placed on the reserve. Although their training includes weapons training there is no evidence that it is anything but defensive.

Those who join the army as a career under the 1972 law are trained at eight colleges that have courses in military science education. The national defense law emphasizes that male and female citizens have the right and obligation to participate in military training in order to understand modern warfare, to improve their skills, and to be able to defend the motherland under combat conditions. The rationale is that every citizen has the "holy duty" to defend the country. Apparently, since the inception of this law, there have been more applicants than positions available in the army, and also many age-waiver requests.

The requirements are that individuals should be between the ages of eighteen and thirty, members of either the Communist party or the workers' youth organization, residents of one of the eight cities where the colleges are located, and high school graduates with good grades; they should have some work experience, no children under one year, and no criminal record. They also have to pass an entrance exam.

Yugoslavia

PARTICIPATION IN TIME OF CONFLICT. Scant information is available on women in the military establishment. What is available deals with World War II. President Tito intimated in a January 1976 interview that more than 100,000 women fought; 90 were proclaimed national heroes; 1,900 were awarded the 1941 memorial plaque; 2,000 were officers; 40,000 were wounded, 3,000 of whom were seriously disabled; and approximately 25,000 died in the fighting ranks.

Countries in Asia and Australasia

Australia and New Zealand

CURRENT PARTICIPATION. Both countries are considering expanding the range of assignments open to women in their armed forces, but neither expects to conscript women or assign them to combat jobs. In 1976 women constituted 5.0 and 5.8 percent of the Australian and New Zealand forces, respectively. In Australia there were 3,508 women (1,550 in the army, 808 in the navy, and 1,050 in the air force) in a total defense force of close to 70,000. In New Zealand the figures were 731 women (279 in the army, 127 in the navy, and 325 in the air force) in a force of about 12,500.

PARTICIPATION IN TIME OF CONFLICT. Australia and New Zealand both had many men and women under arms during World War II.

Originally, New Zealand had only a women's war service auxiliary (a civilian organization), but the increasing threat from Japan in the Pacific, coupled with a decision to retain an expeditionary force in the Middle East, made it necessary to enlist women in all branches of the armed forces. Women in both countries had similar histories to that in the United Kingdom. At the beginning they replaced manpower in purely administrative jobs but later their assignments included torpedo servicing and manning coastal defenses antiaircraft batteries, and the like. Indeed, by the end of the war women were performing every job not beyond their physical capabilities.

Japan

CURRENT PARTICIPATION. Women did not become part of the military until 1952 when they were allowed to enlist in the ground self-defense forces. They were first limited to administrative duties as clerks, typists, and the like; nurses were admitted in 1968; and in 1974 women were accepted in the maritime and air force self-defense forces. The noncombat jobs in logistics, schools, supply corps, and hospitals were opened to women. In 1976 women constituted about 1 percent of the 235,000 individuals in the Japanese self-defense forces. There were 322 female officers (310 in the army, 6 in the navy, and 6 in the air force) and 2,010 enlisted women (1,767 in the army, 115 in the navy, and 128 in the air force).

All women who volunteer must meet rigid physical standards. Officer candidates must be college graduates and between twenty-two and twenty-six years of age; for noncommissioned officers the upper age limit is thirty-six years and they must also be college graduates. Prospective enlistees must be between eighteen and twenty-five, no educational standards are set. Army terms of enlistment are from two to three years, depending on the skills required; the navy and air force terms are three years.

Basic training ranges from five to twelve weeks, depending on the service, and is followed by technical training. Besides the traditional occupations, women can be assigned to general affairs, accounting, personnel, history education, communications, computers, and supply. While few nontraditional jobs are available, women officers do attend the military academy and have served on the staff of the Japan Defense Academy.

People's Republic of China

CURRENT PARTICIPATION. The planning of defense in China appears to involve the entire population in defense organizations that contribute to the armed forces' mission but technically are not part of it. Women participate extensively in youth and organized militia groups, a kind of reserve force. Very little actual data are available about the numbers in the military or their assignments, but recent visitors indicate that some women are being trained as jet pilots. They are admitted to pilot training academies and films indicate that there might be all-female squadrons in the air force.

Philippines

CURRENT PARTICIPATION. A 1963 act established the women's auxiliary corps in the armed forces but limited participation to 1 percent of manpower strength and established a ratio of one officer to twenty enlisted personnel. Promotion was within the ranks of the women's corps only and the highest rank attainable was that of major. A 1973 amendment made few changes except to require that women serve in the reserve. In 1976 it appeared that women still did not constitute the authorized 1 percent of the 78,000 in the Philippine armed forces.

Republic of China (Taiwan)

CURRENT PARTICIPATION. Women may volunteer for peacetime service and are subject to conscription during emergencies. They can enlist in five categories of service as regular or noncommissioned officers for periods of four or three years. The age range is from eighteen to forty-five. In 1976 there were 12,500 women in the military (including 1,900 nurses)—less than 3 percent of Taiwan's defense force of 470,000.

Women joining the women's army corps (WAC) battalion must be high school graduates and between eighteen and twenty-two years of age. After four months' training, the majority serve in the armed forces as second lieutenants assigned to political education, martial song teaching, or battlefield service. Political warfare officers must spend four years at the Political Warfare College and they serve either in senior positions in the WAC battalion or as instructors and the like in the regular armed services. Nursing officers have to be high school graduates and undergo four years' training at nursing school; they serve as first lieutenants for a term of four years. Nurses, on the other hand, must be junior high school graduates and between the ages of fifteen and twenty on enlistment. They serve three years' apprenticeship in nursing and emerge as second lieutenants assigned to the armed forces. About 8,000 women are recruited for administrative jobs for a period of three years.

Countries in the Middle East

Egypt

CURRENT PARTICIPATION. In Egypt women may volunteer for military service. Their first period of such service is for seven years, renewable for five-year terms. Entrance requirements include passing psychological tests, medical tests, and personal interviews; meeting the age requirements of eighteen to twenty-four years; and single status. Women are employed largely in the medical and administrative fields. But there is also speculation that women play a much broader role than that indicated in the available data.

PARTICIPATION IN TIME OF CONFLICT. While a combat role is not mentioned in the data received, Egyptian women were active in the medical support of their armed forces during the Palestinian war of 1948 and the Suez Canal action in 1956; they played an especially active role in all permissible areas in both the 1967 and 1973 Arab-Israeli wars.

Israel[5]

CURRENT PARTICIPATION. By both Western and Israeli standards, Israel has done well in achieving sexual equality, particularly in the kibbutz and the military. Yet the popular conception of the Israeli woman, weapon in hand, as an equal in combat with her male comrades is based more on myth than reality in Israel today. While there may have been some truth in this impression in the earlier years, women's participation in the armed forces has recently been restricted to the more traditional

5. Information on Israel from Plea Albeck, "The Status of Women in Israel," *The American Journal of Comparative Law,* vol. 20 (Fall 1972), pp. 693–96; Verna J. Dickerson, "The Role of Women in the Defense Force of Israel" (U.S. Army War College, May 1974; processed); Lionel Tiger and Joseph Shepher, *Women in the Kibbutz* (Harcourt Brace Jovanovich, 1975).

roles that are less battle-oriented. In short, the evidence indicates that Israel has been overrated as a model of equality for women in the military.

Israel is one of the few countries where women have been conscripted on a continuous basis. Since 1949 when they reach the age of eighteen both men and women become subject to military conscription; they are also obliged to serve in the Civil Defense Service and in the labor service during emergencies. All laws governing this threefold compulsory service are somewhat more liberal in their application to women in regard to age limits, deferments, and exemptions. For example, the period of active military service is shorter for women than for men—twenty-four months as opposed to thirty-six months (in 1974, the length of service for women was increased from twenty to twenty-four months purportedly because of their important contribution to the war effort), and the upper age limit is lower for women: for active service, twenty-six years as opposed to twenty-nine; for the reserves, thirty-eight as opposed to forty-nine.

Women can be exempted from military service for the following reasons: health, pregnancy, motherhood, marriage before the age of eighteen, and religious conviction. Married women remain subject to reserve-duty call-up. Once on active duty, women's assignments to certain military tasks require their consent. The exemption rate of women for all reasons is said to be in the region of 40 to 50 percent of those eligible. This figure cannot be confirmed, but does appear reasonable in light of the number of women who are married and have children by the age of eighteen, have religious exemptions, or opt for alternative service. Kibbutz women probably fulfill their military duties to a greater extent than the rest of the Israeli female population because they generally marry at a later age.

A 1971 plan made police service a military service alternate. To be eligible a woman must live in or have accommodations in the major participating cities. Her service commitment is three years instead of the two-year term in the military, and she is under civil service authority.

Those women who serve in the Israeli Defense Force are administratively controlled by Chen (an abbreviation of Cheil Nashim, "Women's Army"). The abbreviation Chen, however, means grace or charm in Hebrew and consequently the Chen is often referred to as the Charm Corps. The Chen commander, via various levels of Chen officers, is responsible for the basic training, care, and surveillance of women in all branches of the force. In 1976 women apparently accounted for about 5 percent of the Israeli Defense Force.

Basic training for women includes drill marching, weapons training, first aid, defensive maneuvers using live ammunition, as well as studying subjects dealing with the military, history, and education. Despite such training, combat tasks have virtually disappeared for women today. The assignment of most of the women to the more "feminine" occupations epitomizes a growing entrenchment in and a reversion to military policies of traditional sex roles. (The notable exceptions are the women in Nahal, discussed below.)

After the three-month basic training period Chen women are distributed among various units to become clerks, typists, teleprinters, communicators, drivers, mechanics, and cultural, welfare, and medical workers. They form a part of the military police and in the air force are active in pilot training, such as control tower operators and electronic equipment monitors.

Nahal, an acronym for Noar Halutzi Lohem (Fighting Pioneer Youth), is a special unit in the special defense force. After graduation from high school, members of the various youth movements organize themselves into garinim (nuclei). Each nucleus affiliates with a kibbutz that needs additional manpower; about 30 percent are women. After three to six months' training in the kibbutz they join the army, remaining together as much as the sex-differentiated training permits, and then are assigned to agricultural settlements. The women's basic training is not given by Chen but by the Nahal training base. It is more strenuous, emphasizing weapons training, scouting, patroling, topography, and the like. One reason for the difference in training is that both the men and women share the agricultural and military work in the settlements; both carry weapons within the camp and share armed night watch duty.

After training, each Nahal group is assigned to an agricultural settlement where they undergo agricultural training for from six months to a year. The young men go on to advanced army training and the young women go to the kibbutz to which the whole group has been assigned. When the men complete their army courses, they too join the kibbutz. Both are full working members, the men as active reservists and the women as inactive reservists with no military support.

Because of the collective life style kibbutz women were the backbone of the women's army in the 1960s. They were better equipped than other recruits for camp life. Today, however, they are more individualistic and appear to care more about personal satisfaction. Many see today's third generation "kibbutznik" switching to family togetherness instead of conforming to the more communal pattern of the previous decade.

PARTICIPATION IN TIME OF CONFLICT. The women's role in the Israeli military has its roots in the Haganah, the illegal Jewish army formed before the creation of the state of Israel. In the early 1930s women were accepted into the group and their arms training was with light weapons mainly for personal defense. They were used extensively to transport arms past the "gentlemanly" British soldiers who did not search them for such contraband.

In 1936 began a three-year guerilla war between the Arabs and the Jews. Women pushed for greater participation, and by 1937, there were training courses for women commanders. In World War II women served in British Army units. The Palmach (an abbreviation for plugot mahatz, "commando battalions") was established as a special unit of the Haganah. Some women were in this group from its inception while later groups of the garinim joined them, including girls. The training was strenuous and some young women saw armed combat. They were even parachuted into Nazi-occupied countries to organize Jewish self-defense and revolt.

The experiences of the women during this period are relevant to some of today's questions concerning military women. Even though enlisted women saw battle in mixed units, they received basic training in all-female groups. The rationale was that while the competition between the sexes in basic training overstrained the abilities of both, such competition dissipates in actual battle conditions.

In the first phase of Israel's War of Liberation, one out of every five soldiers was female and they shared equally in both offensive and defensive battle situations, especially in the agricultural settlement areas. In the second phase, all of the illegal military groups united to form the Israeli Defense Force (IDF) and women's roles became less battle-task oriented as the war itself became more defensive.